DATE DUE

MAR 1 7 1998	
mar 30	
April 11	
DEC 1 4 1998	

BRODART — Cat. No. 23-221

DOING
THEIR
SHARE
TO
SAVE
THE
PLANET

Doing Their Share to Save the Planet

■

Children and Environmental Crisis

Donna Lee King

 RUTGERS UNIVERSITY PRESS

NEW BRUNSWICK, NEW JERSEY

Library of Congress Cataloging-in-Publication Data

King, Donna Lee.
   Doing their share to save the planet : children and
environmental crisis / Donna Lee King.
      p. cm.
   Includes bibliographical references and index.
   ISBN 0-8135-2184-X (cloth) — ISBN 0-8135-2185-8 (pbk.)
   1. Environmental sciences—Study and teaching (Elementary)
2. Environmental responsibility.   I. Title.
GE70.K56   1995
363.7—dc20   94-41056
                                            CIP

British Cataloging-in-Publication information available

Published by Rutgers University Press, New Brunswick, New Jersey
Manufactured in the United States of America

For Alexander, and for his
great-great-great-great-grandchildren.
May you inhabit
a humane and hospitable world.

Contents

Acknowledgments
ix

Introduction
1

1
Images of Children in Environmental Crisis
7

2
Selling Environmentalism to Kids
29

3
Children's Concerns about the Planet:
Messages in Their Drawings
55

4
What It Means to Kids to Be Green
73

Conclusion
115

Notes
123

Bibliography
127

Index
133

Acknowledgments

Some of the material in Chapter Two appeared in my article "Captain Planet and the Planeteers: Kids, Environmental Crisis, and Competing Narratives of the New World Order," *The Sociological Quarterly* 35 (1) (1993): 103–120. A version of Chapter Three appeared in Joel Best, ed., *Troubling Children: Studies of Children and Social Problems* (Hawthorne, NY: Aldine de Gruyter, 1994).

While in the process of researching and writing this book, I have ushered my son through infancy and toddlerhood into preschool, I have completed graduate coursework and a doctoral dissertation in sociology, I have commuted long distances to teach sleepy college freshmen at eight o'clock in the morning, and, with my family, I have moved three times in the past four years, most recently a thousand miles south to a new teaching position.

There is no way I could have done this alone.

Barbara Katz Rothman ushered *me* through a tough transition from ambivalent graduate student to committed cultural critic. Her sharp intellect, deep-seated moral compass, apt and witty writing style, and warm and constant friendship are a continuing source of inspiration, admiration, and support.

Stanley Aronowitz and the former Committee for Cultural Studies at the Graduate Center of the City University of New York were instrumental in shaping my thinking about what constitutes knowledge, power, and social analysis. Cindi Katz helped to show me a bridge from cultural studies to the study of children. Sue Fisher and Sharon Stephens read drafts of my manuscript at different stages and provided timely feedback and support. Thanks go as well to former editor in chief Marlie Wasserman and to science editor Karen Reeds at Rutgers University Press for their enthusiasm and support for this project. I would also like to thank my agent, Carol Mann.

My mother, Joy Wright King, sent me clippings about eco-terrorists and told me about Captain Planet. My sisters, Denise King Dunning, Susan King, Lynne Mushock, and their teacher friends helped gather drawings from schoolchildren in South Carolina. Christie Cusa, Terry Ingersoll, Amy Gustafson, and Maryanne, Joan, and Shannon at the New Paltz Methodist Play-school provided quality care for my son while I was busy at my "other" work. And without the tireless support of my husband, Alan Bowden, none of this would have been possible.

I might never have noticed the connection between kids and environmental crisis if not for my son, Alexander. It is to him, and to Alan, that I dedicate this work in loving gratitude.

Wilmington, North Carolina
August 1994

> Nature is a topic of public discourse on which much turns, even the earth.
>
> —Donna Haraway, "The Promises of Monsters"

When the world started, way back when, there were no problems,
no troubles with men.
Then all of a sudden, before too long, things started going wrong.
You had nothing to worry about if you were older; the weight was on the young person's shoulder.
Now, do you really think it's right; that the children should have to win someone else's fight?
We didn't cause this, to the earth we just came.
But already it's time to stop playing this game.
This problem must be stopped *now* before the future generation is forced to have to suffer through all of the frustration.
We must try our hardest to make sure they don't see the great downfall.
And above all the rest, we must remember, there's only one Earth for all.

> —Natalya Scimeca, Eighth-grade schoolgirl and environmental-essay-contest winner

Introduction

Often, crisis themes that arise in one generation are appropriated by society for socializing the next. For baby boomers of the Cold War era, many of whom recall crouching at their desks in classrooms during the Cuban missile crisis, the issue of the time was fallout shelters and the "communist threat." Watching marches in Selma and riots in Watts, children of the fifties and sixties also learned of civil rights and racial strife. In the wake of assassinations and near impeachment of political leaders, nightly newscasts of Vietnam War atrocities, and hostage taking in the Middle East, children of the seventies experienced a collapse of confidence in the American way. Nuclear proliferation resurged in the eighties with Star Wars and Reaganomics, leaving many children plagued with "psychic numbing" and nuclear nightmares.

In the 1990s, the fate of the environment is the most pervasive crisis theme aimed at children. Although children today face the serious problems of poverty, violence, and diminished opportunities for meaningful and well-paid work, these crises receive merely a fraction of the exposure that environmental crisis enjoys in popular media, schools, and virtually every other arena of a child's life. On T-shirts and diapers, animal crackers and Burger King bags, in classrooms and on cartoons, a persistent call for children to save the planet is promoted and embraced. British scholar and essayist Rosalind Coward notes that "children and ecology are two terms that seem to go naturally together. Much green rhetoric is about our children's future" (1990:40).

The current emphasis on children and environmental crisis contains some unique features that distinguish it from past crises and crusades. Not only a cause and concern, "saving the planet" is also a *culture,* both material and nonmaterial. It is a way of life, a set of social practices, a symbolic system, and a contested political terrain. This book is about how children fit into the complex culture of environmentalism, and the social, emotional, and political implications this culture entails.

My induction into the culture of children and environmental crisis occurred in the fall of 1990, in the months following the twentieth-anniversary celebration of Earth Day. Seated in an overstuffed rocker while nursing my infant son, I found myself watching children's television programming for the first time. Snippets of *Sesame Street, Mister Rogers, Reading Rainbow,* and the like, were among my daily fare. But it was an environmental-essay contest repeatedly broadcast on our local public-television station during those autumn months that left a powerful impression upon me. Every day, morning and after-noon, I watched schoolchildren read essays, recite poems, and show pictures about "why we should save the earth."[1] Typical of these children was a small first-grade boy, standing alone on the dark screen, explaining, "The earth is dying. We should save the earth for the trees. We have to save it. It is going to waste. There is no other planet to go to. If we don't stop polluting it, we and everybody will die."

Perhaps in part because I was experiencing, as a new mother, a heightened sense of receptivity to children and their vulnera-bility, I found these images of disaster—emanating from the hands and mouths of babes—overwhelming. And it was then that I began to consider what the culture of environmental crisis might mean to *children,* a social category by definition power-less in myriad ways. Telling children to save the planet seemed utterly contradictory, yet everywhere I looked, the message was going out to kids that their job is to solve environmental crisis.

But at the same time that images of ecological disaster per-vade children's cultural landscape, so do simple environmental "solutions." John Javna's enormously popular book *50 Simple Things Kids Can Do to Save the Earth* provides a good example. Taken from the perspective of this genre, environmental crisis becomes not overwhelming and seemingly insurmountable, but upbeat, easy, and even fun. Children are told to turn off the lights, read by a window, recycle cans, and shop for an energy-efficient car. I began to understand why it is so easy for adults to be enthusiastic about environmentalizing kids:

> Americans . . . are ready to embrace green (particularly when it comes to an outdoor concert or two), to take it into their hearts and homes, to testify that making a difference—whether by using cloth diapers or by separating cans from bottles—has changed their lives. Who could argue? Feeling powerful (and righteous to boot) is a rare and delicious commodity these days; besides it takes an unseemly streak of perversity to be *against* the environment. (Bolotin 1990:47)

Mixed into this cultural brew of children, disaster, and simple "empowering" solutions is another important ingredient that demands careful consideration: the *selling* of environmental crisis to kids. When I first started thinking about children and environmental crisis, I asked an acquaintance from Germany, a young woman in her midtwenties, whether she recalled the Green party influencing the culture of German children in the late 1970s and early 1980s. She answered that the Greens were more a political phenomenon than a cultural one, and that they did not target children. She explained that German children might be involved in environmentalism if their parents were active environmentalists, but she knew of no children's culture of environmental crisis.

In the United States of the 1990s, quite the opposite is the case. Cultural and commercial aspects of environmentalism dominate, and children are aggressively targeted as a consumer market for "green" products; they are exploited as social icons and political symbols in all manner of environmental media; and they are systematically told, by the popular culture as much as if not more than in the schools, that they must "save the planet."

This popular culture of environmental crisis, with its apparent contrast to the more overtly political model of the German Greens, raises a number of questions of social and political significance: What is the social meaning of children as targets of environmental messages? as environmental icons? as environmental actors? What is revealed about late-twentieth-century American society by the intersection of culture, commerce, and the environmentalization of children? Which ideological underpinnings support liberal environmentalism, and how do children negotiate what I believe to be a contradictory political/environmental stance? Is environmentalism simply another form of social reproduction, by which children are subtly coerced into consensus and efficiently incorporated into the existing social structure—in this instance through the appropriation of environmentalist rhetoric? Or do children find spaces in this rhetoric for effective expressions of political empowerment?

This book is a study of children and environmentalism in the United States today. It is based on research I conducted from 1990 through 1993 in upstate New York and in South Carolina on children, culture, and environmental crisis. The first two chapters focus on the culture of children and environmental crisis. In them I analyze artifacts of mass-mediated environmental culture: images, texts, messages, material objects, signs. In Chapter One I look at various and contradictory images of children in environmental media—noble savages, vulnerable victims, political pawns, ecofascists—and I discuss the political and ideological subtexts underpinning these representations. In Chapter Two I explore where in the popular culture children learn about environmental crisis and what kinds of messages they are getting about saving the planet. I use a popular environmental cartoon for children, *Captain Planet and the Planeteers,* to demonstrate fundamental contradictions inherent in the mass marketing of environmentalism to kids, contradictions I call a "liberal-environmental paradox." The liberal-environmental paradox includes a simultaneous call for children (and others) both to conserve and to consume; a diffusion of responsibility that supports the notion that environmental crisis is everyone's fault; and simple, individual "lifestyle" solutions to complex social-structural problems of global proportions. I argue that in its rhetoric, liberal environmentalism unreflectively reproduces the ideologies and social relations of patriarchy, racism, and capitalism that are at the root of the very problems it supposedly seeks to change.

The second half of the book is based on interviews, drawings, essays, and participant observation I conducted with children at schools, playgrounds, summer camps, and in neighborhoods.

Here I explore children's *experience* of environmental crisis, what "being green" means to them. In Chapter Three I look at children's drawings of saving the planet and formulate different categories of children's environmental concern. In Chapter Four I talk with children about their thoughts and feelings about environmental crisis and look at what children do (or would if they could) about saving the planet.

Virtually all children in the United States have heard about environmental crisis. Some experience hopelessness and despair, particularly those already disenfranchised groups such as poor black children and girls. But many more children—girls and boys, black and white, gifted and "special education"—have developed a clear sense of empowerment, a buoyant belief that they can do something about the problem. However, how empowering is it to teach children about radioactive waste or massive destruction of rainforests and then tell them the answer is to plant a tree in the backyard or to pick up litter? In the conclusion I explore this as a complex and problematic kind of environmental "empowerment" in need of careful and critical attention. My basic premise is that the environmentalization of children is a social and political practice that is filled with conflicting notions of who our children are and what their powers and responsibilities will be in the future. My hope is that this work will contribute to a meaningful debate about the role of children in environmental crisis, and ultimately to a new world of a different order than the one children must deal with today.

1

■

Images
of Children
in Environmental
Crisis

Consider four portraits of children and the environment:

■ With its colorful pictures of rugged landscapes and expensive socks, the Patagonia outdoor clothing catalog is a model of upscale nature gear marketing. A winter catalog includes a lengthy essay featuring poet Gary Snyder, active environmentalist and longtime wilderness advocate, who says this about children and environmental crisis:

> The practice of the wild refines our thinking about the wild, extending it beyond the realm of vacation spots, beyond the facts and equations of scientific explanation, to a place familiar to any child who persists in asking, "Why?" Children know that natural metaphors of plants and animals penetrate to the wild place, that fairy tales are true, that *they are little animals*. That is why they so vigorously oppose the forces of domesticity and civilized education. They know quite well they would be better off in the forests, the mountains, the deserts, and the seas. (Turner 1994:49, my emphasis)

■ Maria V. Cherkasova, a university-trained biologist and director of the Center for Independent Ecological Programs in Moscow, specialized in rare and endangered birds of the Altai Mountain region until she began to study the impact of chemical and radioactive contamination on the health of the Russian population, particularly its children. Regarding children and environmental crisis, she notes:

> Health conditions of the children of early and school ages is also evidently becoming worse. The most alarming is the growing number of cancer[s] among children. Nearly all the children are suffering from allergies. Over the last five years occurrence of [bronchial] asthma has increased in Russia 1.5 times. All in all, more than half of Russia's children have poor health.... Being a specialist in rare and endangered species I may with full responsibility state that Russia's population (at least in some regions) is in the process of dying out. (n.d.:2)

■ The politically conservative journal *Policy Review,* published an article by Jonathan Adler entitled "Little Green Lies: The Environmental Miseducation of America's Children." Adler, an environmental-policy analyst at the Competitive Enterprise Institute in Washington, D.C. writes:

> While environmentalism is likely to be a mainstay of education in the years to come, this does not mean that America's children are to be condemned to curricula of half-truths and political advocacy. Instead, children can, and should, be taught *facts, not conjecture,* and they should learn the whole story, including how an environmental concern fits into the greater ecological and *economic context....* Environmental education can be a valuable addition to school curricula, but only if it is conducted in a careful, thoughtful, *and nonideological manner.* After all, schools are for education, *not political indoctrination.* (1992:18–26, my emphasis)

■ On the August 9–11, 1991, cover of a *USA Weekend Magazine,* distributed to over thirty-four-million readers, stand three children of three different ethnicities, identically clad in black T-shirts, blue jeans, and dark, impenetrable, black sunglasses. The headline reads, "The Enforcers: A New Breed of Kid Is Getting Tough on Parents Who Let the Water Run, Wear Fur,

Don't Recycle or Otherwise Flout Their '60s Values." In a letter to the editor, a reader responds:

> If your cover photo was supposed to amuse me, it failed. It frightened me. There are those of us who can remember Hitler and Stalin and how they used kids to spy on and coerce parents to carry out their political schemes. The environmental movement goes far beyond protecting Mother Earth from human beings. Its political overtones (or undertones) are manifested on your cover. (*USA Weekend Magazine* 1991)

A feature article in the home section of *The New York Times* runs with the headline "Newest Parental Nightmare: Eco-Smart Child," and reports:

> In the old days, the children were the sneaky ones— smoking in the bathroom and doing other things they shouldn't. Now, it's the parents who are afraid of being caught by their environmentally aware, health-conscious and "politically-correct" children, some of whom are barely out of kindergarten. . . . These vociferous children are harassing their parents to save water, forget about diet soda, keep away from red meat, abandon fur coats, stop smoking and shut off the lights. They also insist on paying attention to the new recycling laws, no matter what. No wonder there is quite a number of parents who, having put their little darlings on the bus to summer camp, are breathing a sigh of relief. (Slesin 1991)

Little animals, endangered species, political pawns, parental nightmares—each portrait of children and environmental crisis tells a different story and can be read in a number of ways. Where do these images come from and what can they tell us about children, nature, and late-twentieth-century society? To understand the disparate and often disparaging images in the popular culture of children and environmental crisis, we must first recognize that childhood and nature are not simply natural categories but are also social constructions located within specific historical and cultural contexts.

The "Discovery" of Childhood

Debates over the meaning of children and childhood have existed in the social sciences for several decades. French cultural historian Phillipe Ariès is widely credited with the "discovery of childhood." In his classic study *Centuries of Childhood,* Ariès makes the bold assertion that "in medieval society the idea of childhood did not exist" (1962:125). Basing his analysis on medieval paintings, in which European children are depicted as "miniature adults," Ariès concludes that children as a social category did not exist before the fifteenth century. Infants, says Ariès, nursed at their mothers' breast until between the ages of five and seven years, at which point they were weaned and then "immediately absorbed into the world of adults" (329). Children who passed into the adult world were accorded no special status and, as such, experienced no special restrictions. They participated in every aspect of adult society, including work, play, and war.

But with the advent of moral pedagogy (beginning in the fifteenth century and culminating in the eighteenth) childhood ultimately came to be conceived as a unique period of innocence and weakness (both moral and physical) requiring strict adult intervention and institutional supervision, first by the church and then by the schools (333).

While education initially was a project for the upper and then middle classes, eventually even lower-class children were "saved" from the adult world of work and the streets. In the United States, by the early 1900s virtually all children were brought (though not without a bitter social struggle) into the fold of a "normal" childhood, one in which children were at once economically unproductive and emotionally precious (Zelizer 1985).

Toward the end of the twentieth century, concern in the United States has shifted to the "disappearance" of childhood. Children are said to be "hurried" into adulthood by day care, divorce, violence, and too much television viewing. The image of children as vulnerable to kidnapping, sadism, and sexual abuse has received widespread media coverage (cf. Best 1990; Lynott and Logue 1993).

While these accounts of childhood are interesting and provocative, buried within them are white, Western, and patriarchal assumptions that need to be excavated and explained. Sociologist and childbirth scholar Barbara Katz Rothman compares the discovery of childhood with other discoveries by Western explorers: "As men of a certain class, place, and race traveled somewhere for the first time, it became 'discovered.' Never mind that others were living in that land for eternities" (Simonds and Rothman 1992:254). Ariès's account, says Katz Rothman, ignores the unique relationship between women and babies, denies the sociality of infant life, and implies that children under the care of their mothers and nannies were not in the company of "adults" (254–55).

Similarly, accounts of hurried children and eroded childhood romanticize the past and ignore race, class, and gender differences that have always shaped children's experiences and limited their life chances; furthermore, these romanticized ideals lay blame on women who work outside the home, use day care, or raise children alone.

Defining childhood and determining who gets to define "the child" are not simple or straightforward matters; they are historically specific and politically charged. In the restructuring of late-twentieth-century global society—postindustrial, postmodern, and environmentally challenged—analysis of contradictory images of children and environmental crisis can provide entry into the contested political and cultural terrain of childhood, nature, and global society.

Little Animals and Noble Savages

Michael Moore's 1989 documentary *Roger & Me,* a sad and funny tale of postindustrial decline in Flint, Michigan—the direct result of the ruthless corporate practices of General Motors—contains a memorable sequence of scenes about rabbits. Among the many people we meet in the film, struggling to eke out a living in Flint after the mass closing of GM plants in and around the city, is a scrawny, young woman who raises rabbits. In her yard hangs a sign that reads Pets or Meat. Moore explores the implications in this sign throughout the film when he queries the woman directly about its meaning ("If you can't sell 'em as pets, you've gotta get rid of 'em as meat," she responds) and even more graphically when he films the young woman clubbing and then gutting and skinning a big, furry "fryer." Later, in a lesser-known sequel entitled *Pets or Meat?* (a Dog Eat Dog production), Moore returns to visit the young woman, whose name we learn is Rhonda. Rhonda is now a new mother, working part-time at K-Mart, her entire wages, sixty dollars and change, garnished every week by the U.S. bankruptcy court. When we see her last she is trying to make ends meet by raising rabbits and rats for pet snake meat.

The sign Pets or Meat has stayed with me since I first saw Moore's movie, and I use the film often in my sociology classes to describe the human costs of capital flight. But while studying children and environmental crisis, a new association occurred to me in the popular depiction of children as little animals and noble savages. Recall Gary Snyder's characterization of children:

> Children know that natural metaphors of plants and animals penetrate to the wild place, that fairy tales are true, that *they are little animals.* That is why they so vigorously oppose the forces of domesticity and civilized education. They know quite well they would be better off in the forests, the mountains, the deserts, and the seas. (Turner 1994:49)

The notion of children as "little animals" naturally in touch with nature and the earth is central to twentieth-century Western constructions of the child. Ariès lays the foundation at the feet of eighteenth-century Genevan philosopher Jean Jacques Rousseau: "The association of childhood with primitivism and irrationalism or prelogicism characterizes our contemporary conception of childhood. This concept made its appearance in Rousseau, but it belongs to twentieth-century history" (Ariès 1962:119). Although Lucio Colletti (1972) persuasively rejects commonplace notions that Rousseau advocated the abolishment of society and a "return again to the forests to live among the bears,"[1] the point remains: children are frequently depicted as romantic "noble savages," and this is evident in environmental discourse today.

One common strategy uses images of children as aesthetic

objects, to exude a sensual as well as emotional appeal. This is not unlike popular advertisements for the United Colors of Benetton, or Gap Kids, in which beautiful children of every hue are photographed in luscious, full-color detail. These images are designed to please both eye and heart. They are meant to sell not only clothing but a subtext that seemingly resolves (and certainly exploits) issues of racism through the power of aesthetic presentation. An example of this technique applied to environmentalism can be found in a sentimental music video featuring Bette Midler (an entertainer who began her career performing topless in gay bathhouses). Filmed in black and white to achieve a dreamlike or fantasy effect, the video depicts children dressed in hyper-romantic costume. A white girl in a black dress and oversized blonde wig sits in a field, quietly painting a picture of the planet earth. A boy dressed in feathers and beak peeks at her from behind a tree, while children made up as wood sprites and ragamuffins roam countryside and town, aiding the disadvantaged and interceding in mock conflicts. Accompanied by a thematic refrain, "God is watching us from a distance . . . this song is for Everyman," the message is clear—if only adults could be more like (idealized) children and attend to the will of an absent yet all-powerful Father, everything would be all right.

Romantic images of children as little animals and noble savages contain deep contradictions. This became apparent during the 1992 Earth Summit in Rio, where the different depiction and treatment of First World and Third World children revealed subtle hierarchies of race, region, and development (Stephens 1992). The UNICEF ship *Gaia* carried an international group of children from Norway to Rio under a banner that urged, Keep the Promise for a Better World for *All* the Children. *Time* magazine queried, "What kind of planet will our children inherit?" and included a photo spread of a pristine landscape with a small child's figure in the foreground.[2] Similar images and sentiments about children were rampant in media coverage of the international environmental event.

But masked by cavalier rhetoric about "*all* the world's children" are global social inequalities that are subtly stated yet grossly obvious in the contrasting depictions and treatments of First World and Third World children. *Newsweek* magazine's

Earth Summit coverage featured a group photograph of "the world's children" that placed children from South America, Africa, and Asia behind children from North America, Europe, and Australia. Even starker was the cover of *The Economist* magazine's special Rio issue: a full-frame photograph of a mass of Rwandan schoolboys, overlaid with the words, "The question Rio forgets," to raise the specter of "population explosion."

As anthropologist and child researcher Sharon Stephens notes:

> Media images of masses of hungry Third World children, set beside images of healthy, happy children in pristine, uncrowded environments, can be used to suggest—at a level "behind" or "beneath" the verbal arguments being made—that the cost of a clean environment for "our children" is the labelling of other people's children as "excess populations." It is . . . important to note that the children representing "Third World overpopulation" are . . . always black, even though many Third World nations are Asian, and of course many of the world's poor are white. There is a disturbing racist aspect to international media illustrations of "overpopulation." (1992:51)

Even more egregious inequities than racist representations may have occurred to Third World children in Rio during the Earth Summit. Environmental writer and journalist Benjamin A. Goldman reports that the ecological camp where the good ship *Gaia* docked was allegedly built by the forced labor of Brazilian street children. Organizers of the *Gaia* camp were sued for violating child labor laws. And it is estimated that as many as one thousand street children in Rio may have been "swept up" in the months before the Earth Summit in a "cleanup" led by the Brazilian military (Goldman 1992:10–11).

Children portrayed and understood as little animals or noble savages are at risk for poor treatment by their masters, as pets, as pests, or as meat. Western ambivalence toward "savages" is captured in an article on the poisoning of the Pacific Rim and its peoples by the nuclear West:

> The records of a 1956 U.S. Atomic Energy Commission briefing note that one AEC official characterized the Mar-

shall Islands as "by far one of the most contaminated areas in the world," then suggested that their residents were preferable as test subjects to the mice often used in laboratory experiments: "While it is true that these people do not live, I would say, the way Westerners do, civilized people, it is nevertheless true that they are more like us than mice." (Walters 1992:35)

With an ethos such as this informing our cultural and political landscapes, we need to look closely and cautiously at poetic visions of children as little animals and noble savages who know they are better off in the forests, the mountains, the deserts, and the seas.

Endangered Species: Children at Environmental Risk

Around the world children are at risk as a direct result of environmental crisis. In the Upper Silesia region of Poland, the air is so toxic from coal-burning factories and leaded gasoline that schoolchildren must stay indoors during recess. The only fresh produce available to them, locally grown fruits and vegetables, is contaminated with arsenic, lead, and other posionous heavy metals accumulated in the soil.

Alarmingly high rates of childhood leukemia, lead poisoning, upper-respiratory distress, mental retardation, and infant mortality are reported throughout Eastern Europe. Recognizing the ecological risks, some women are delaying childbearing "until the environment gets better" (Fischoff 1991:17).

In the aftermath of the 1986 Chernobyl disaster, children throughout Russia and Europe played in the nuclear rain of the March meltdown, while mothers struggled in vain to find milk, meat, and produce that were not potentially irradiated (Hirsh 1994). In another kind of deadly play, in Brazil's central state of Goiás, in 1987, street children found an old cancer therapy machine in an abandoned house. As many as ten thousand people may have been contaminated after exposure to its attractive glowing blue contents—radioactive cesium 137. One little girl became so irradiated after eating the metal dust that she glowed blue in the night and had to be buried in a lead coffin (Goldman and Goldman 1992).

Similarly, in the wake of the 1990 Gulf War, children in Basra, Iraq, played hand puppets with empty U.S. artillery shells made of "depleted" uranium. This game is suspected of causing a dramatic increase in childhood cancers and mysterious swollen abdomens in Iraqi children (Hoskins, quoted in Stephens 1994).

Even more horrific, in what feminist environmentalist Joni Seager ironically labels a "designer tragedy," a Swiss television crew said it found evidence that the Ciba–Geigy corporation, one of the world's largest chemical manufacturers, intentionally sprayed unprotected Egyptian children with a new insecticide that the conglomerate was introducing in the early 1980s. As Seager reports, "The purpose of the experiment apparently was to see how much of the insecticide was retained in the human body and how much was excreted" (1993:73).

In the United States, poor children and children of color are more likely to live and play near incinerators, landfills, toxic-waste dumps, and agribusinesses, sharply increasing their exposure to pesticides, toxic leaks, airborne pollution particles, and heavy-metal contamination. Disproportionately high rates of lung disease, lead poisoning, asthma, cancer, mental retardation, and learning disabilities are reported among poor and minority children in the United States, in a situation many characterize as environmental racism (Bullard 1990; "Home Street, U.S.A." 1991).

Vulnerable Children as Environmental Icons

Children are indeed victims of environmental crisis. But the portrayal of children as vulnerable victims finds many different expressions in popular rhetoric for, and against, environmentalism. In contradictory and complex ways, children are used as social icons and political symbols in environmental messages about saving the planet.

The most common theme is a cautionary one, describing a

morbid legacy of environmental degradation and pollution bequeathed by adults to the young. Environmentalists, seeking to raise popular consciousness and instill proper ecological behavior, invoke parental responsibility for protecting the vital interests of the next generation. "I don't want my children to grow up in a world that is covered with Styrofoam," states a celebrity model on a 1991 Earth Day cable television extravaganza. In a music video about picking up trash, a voice-over declares, "I want my kids to have a clean planet Earth." "We recycle for Pete's sake. And Susie's. And Billy's," a Target Stores promotional handout intones.

Children as an abstract, universal class are portrayed facing rapidly diminishing resources. The theme reflects notions of inheritance, of "responsibility for future generations." But as we have seen, not *all* the world's children are slotted for the same inheritance, despite the rhetoric of universal concern.

Visual images of children at risk are a powerful, emotional means of expressing environmental messages. On the same cable television Earth Day celebration, fifteen-second promotional clips of a documentary about the Savannah River nuclear-weapons facility were broadcast. Over and over in ominous tones the announcer recited, "Coming up, *Building Bombs,* a one-hour documentary about the deadly effects of making weapons." Each time the word "deadly" was intoned, the video cut to a babbling brook where a young father helps a tow-headed toddler drink water seemingly drawn from the brook. Innocuous in any other context, here the activity of a child drinking water is associated with contamination from radioactive waste. The unwitting poisoning of innocent babes—by their fathers no less, is an image meant to cut to the core of deep-seated anxieties about the protection and preservation of the young.

Children's vulnerability is viewed by many adults across the political spectrum as a cause of great concern, and this concern is exploited in liberal environmental campaigns. A *Mother Jones* magazine pullout called the "Toxic Ten: America's Truant Corporations," prominently features a color photograph of a well-dressed Asian boy in striped pants, suspenders, cap, and white hospital mask that covers the little boy's entire face but his distressed gaze. The caption reads: "A three-year old leukemia victim in California's Central Valley, where heavy pesticide use has been linked to high rates of childhood cancers, spends his afternoons in a treatment clinic." On the next page is a smaller picture of a fair-haired, white-skinned toddler girl in a two-piece bathing suit, holding sunglasses and an inflatable swimming tube above the caption "Ozone Hole." The caption goes on to indict the Du Pont, General Motors, and Rockwell corporations as "major sources of chemicals that eat our atmosphere" ("Toxic Ten" 1993).

The use of children as political icons was an openly acknowledged strategy of the antinuclear movement of the late 1970s and 1980s. Writing about the impact of nuclear proliferation on children, antinuclear activist, Phyllis La Farge discusses the "inspiration of the child." Children, she says, are an inspiration to political activism in parents "political action [is] part of mothering," and intimate contact with children is seen as a politically sensitizing experience, available not only to women but to "more and more men" (1987:127). The goal of the antinuclear movement was to raise public consciousness about the dangers of nuclear proliferation by making children's vulnerability a central issue.[3] Antinuclear activists strategically used images of vulnerable children to promote their political aim. Pamphlets entitled *What About the Children* were distributed to exert pressure on local school boards to detail nonexistent evacuation plans in the event of nuclear war, forcing public recognition of the vulnerability of children to mass nuclear destruction. As La Farge states, "Clearly, this strategy, which spoke to officials in their role *in loco parentis,* had at its core the image of the child" (1987:143).

Another strategy involved actively recruiting children into antinuclear organizations. A "complex motivation" was at work, according to La Farge, that included helping children "deal with" the nuclear issue, and getting children involved in antinuclear activism. (1987:144). Mobilization of public opinion was effected by using real children as a "visible" presence at rallies and marches and at public-relations events. The tactic was seen as problematic by many even within the antinuclear movement, however, in part because of the implicit exploitation of children for their symbolic value but also because adults were perceived as "unloading" the problem of nuclear proliferation on children, telling kids, in effect, "This is really your issue" (1987:145).

Vulnerable Victims and Political Pawns

Within the environmental movement there is also concern about dumping adult problems on children's shoulders and recruiting children in environmental campaigns. It is a complex concern, rife with contradictions, and it takes many different political forms.

Mothering magazine decries the "heavy load" that saving the planet places on children and indicts adults for passing the burden to the young:

> How many children are already overwhelmed by well-intentioned campaigns to provide education on ozone, the greenhouse effect, and other serious environmental disturbances? Which of today's Earth in Crisis messages encourage our children to act? Which ones are scary and debilitating? How do we adults come across to children—as a population bent on ditching its responsibility to model appropriate lifestyles? Are we attempting to pass the burden on to *their* generation? (Yasi 1993:99)

Concern for the state of children's emotions and their potential environmental overload is prominent here. The solution often proposed is to foster a sense of "ecological well-being" in children—both by encouraging adults to take environmental responsibility and by helping children to feel they are up to the environmental task they face. Environmental activism is presented as a "lifestyle" issue, and emotional empowerment of children is a prominent goal; small daily activities that children can perform, such as recycling bottles or picking up litter, are encouraged as positive and validating experiences. In this way, according to *Mothering,* children are said to be provided with "a kind of faith that will give rise to a tireless environmentalis[m]" (Yasi 1993:99).

The image of children as burdened by environmental demands and overwhelmed by apocalyptic rhetoric is also a subject for humorists. Stand-up comic Steve Wright performs a wry routine as an overwrought, bleary-eyed, sleepless little boy, up night after night because Smokey the Bear has told him, "Only *you* can prevent forest fires!" In the popular comic strip "Calvin and Hobbes," another little boy, Calvin, is angry at finding trash dumped in the woods. He complains to his imaginary tiger friend Hobbes, "I don't understand why humans evolved as such thoughtless, shortsighted creatures." "Well," says Hobbes, "it can't stay that way forever." "You think we'll get smarter?" Calvin asks hopefully. "That's one of two possibilities," replies the pragmatic Hobbes. In a poignant frame, little Calvin is shown alone in the act of unpleasant epiphany. Next frame he states, *"Maybe we'll stop before it's too late."* "We're all holding our breath," Hobbes retorts (Watterson 1994).

The image of children overburdened by adult concerns takes on a completely different hue when "political indoctrination" in environmental education is introduced as a problem. "Let Kids Be Kids," writes Stephen Hicks in a *Wall Street Journal* article reprinted and widely circulated in a condensed version in the blandly popular and politically conservative *Reader's Digest.*

> Children are not able to deal with global environmental concerns when they are still grappling with personal hygiene. . . . Don't overburden them with *political* problems when they're still learning to solve their own. . . . When we overload [children] with such problems, they become frightened and frustrated. If a teacher persists, students simply mouth the appropriate words to appease them. (1991:129, my emphasis)

While children's emotional well-being is again a professed concern, children here are depicted as vulnerable to a new and insidious danger, "political correctness" dictated by liberal teachers and environmental zealots. This is reminiscent of Adler's charge that innocent children are being indoctrinated by environmental activists into "curricula of half-truths and political advocacy." For Adler and other anti-environmentalists, however, the *real* danger, is not the manipulation of naive children but rather, potential environmental regulations that might impede the "free" accumulation of capital. In the conclusion of his essay, entitled "Towards a Better Shade of Green," Adler uses a rhetoric of concern for children and the environment, but the "green" he is referring to is the color of money:

Children need to be taught that there are trade-offs implicit in every environmental issue.... Environmental regulations can often have significant impacts upon regional and national economies, yet wealthier nations are not only healthier, but also more likely to be concerned about the environment. This too should be an important consideration.... If educators approach environmental issues in such a balanced fashion, our children might not turn out politically-correct, but at least they will be much more "eco-smart." (1992:26)

The political recruitment of children in the environmental debate raises complex and disturbing questions about who holds, and what are, the "best interests of the child." Children are portrayed as vulnerable, innocent victims essentially helpless in the face of global disaster. Yet, at the same time, children are recruited and displayed in environmental activism and told they can do something about the problems with which they are faced.

Liberals worry about childhood burnout and emotional distress while they bombard children with images of environmental disaster and recruit children to environmental campaigns to save the earth. Conservatives charge that children are used as political pawns to advance the radical agendas of environmental activists even as they exploit emotional images of vulnerable children to achieve their own narrow political ends. With accusations flying across the political spectrum, one thing is certain: children are being used.

The problem of overburdened and exploited children is addressed from a completely different perspective in a 1991 *Palm Beach Post* editorial cartoon (Wright 1991) published around the time of the arrest of children's entertainer Pee Wee Herman for masturbating in the sticky darkness of an X-rated movie theater in Florida.

"Son, about Pee Wee Herman," says the father in the first frame of the cartoon. "Yes! We want to help you through this crisis," adds the mother. In the following three frames, the child, drawn very small in relation to his extremely tall parents, responds:

Pee Wee Herman? I'm facing a future plagued with AIDS, a dying, dirty planet, decaying cities, crime, drugs, stifling debt, guns, substandard education, dumb courts and a shredded constitution! Did Pee Wee Herman do *that?* No! It happened while you grown-ups sat on your backsides reading sex trivia! Frankly, you disgust me! Now go to your room!

Here a reversal of generational roles is used to depict a child more adult-like than many American adults, particularly in his sophisticated, if pessimistic, political outlook. Unlike children depicted as political naifs still mastering personal hygiene, child here exceeds parent in his analysis of crisis and political priorities. His disgust at his parents' prurient interest and his impassioned inventory of contemporary social crises imply not only a mature insight into political affairs but also tolerance for varied expressions of sexual desire.

This is a different kind of child, one seemingly savvy and committed, vocally expressive and politically active, emotionally and intellectually mature. It is an image that strikes fear into the hearts of many adults.

Environmental Enforcers

Adult anxiety is palpable in the progression from images of children as beautifully or vulnerably innocent, through portrayals of children as unfairly burdened by adult concerns, to representations of the adultlike child, wise beyond her years. Among these, it is only the politically savvy and passionately informed child who is perceived as a threat and who is therefore the most ambivalently portrayed. This ambivalence is exemplified in popular representations of children as environmental tyrants.

Wrapped in the cloak of the ecotyrant are children who "bully" their parents into recycling, who "shame" their parents into giving up alcohol, cigarettes, meat, and furs. The litany of descriptions applied by the popular press to environmentally concerned children is extensive and homologous: "nagging," "harassing," "tormenting," "vociferous," "proselytizers," "crusaders," "green police." Together they form a compendium of negative labels that conjure up ominous visions of cult worship and political fanaticism.

At the same time, many of these popular representations of children as environmental activists convey ambivalent and complex messages. Often a tone of parental indulgence can be detected, as toward a pampered and precocious pet.

> For Michael Clement, the memory of a recent encounter with his 6-year-old is still vivid. "One morning I was in the bathroom brushing my teeth. Carolyn walked in and quietly shut off the water. Then, calmly, she said, 'Daddy, don't you care about the earth?' " The Arizona father and doctor, equal parts amused and amazed by his daughter's eco-awareness, had no good answer. Now he has taken to wondering each day what orders await him from the girl he and his wife have begun calling "Miss Ecology 1991." The bottom line: He's stopped running water unnecessarily. "It's hard to argue with a charming little girl, especially when you know she's right." (Garelik 1991:4)

Invariably mixed with parents' rueful respect, however, is a fair bit of annoyance with the "ecosmart" child. Children are said to be earnest and stern ecotaskmasters, while parents are portrayed as self-indulgent, silly, and beleaguered by their progeny.

> It's a reversal of the age-old generational war: now children are bullying their parents into changing their behavior. (Better 1992)

> "She's harassing me, that child," said an exasperated [mother]. "If I leave the water on when I'm brushing my teeth, she yells at me. She says, 'Off, off, off. You're wasting that water.' " (Boccella 1991)

> "It's bad enough when your mother did it to you. Now the kids are on to us." (Slesin 1991)

> "The kids are right, but I'd like to make my own decisions in life." (Garelik 1991).

Parents of the "1960s generation" in particular are singled out as having lost (or never really had) an environmental conscience.

> The parents who were peaceniks, or otherwise politi-
> cally active and socially conscious in the 60's seem to be
> on the shortest fuses. [One] self-avowed "sympathizer to
> the antiwar movement" hates that she cannot take a bath
> in peace.... "[M]y daughter ... tells me I'm wasting wa-
> ter. It drives me crazy." (Slesin 1991) Parents . . . are
> taken aback by their younger children's concerns. It's as
> though the soundtrack of their own '60s youths (Save
> this! Stop that!) has been programmed into their off-
> spring, with perhaps more emphasis on actually doing
> something, not just protesting. (Garelik 1991).

In these popular reports children frequently explain that the recalcitrance of ecologically wayward parents results from the parents' never having learned about the environment in school.

> [One child] blames the blunder, in part, on the genera-
> tion gap. "If my parents had seen the program on TV,
> they would have said, 'That's too bad about the dolphins,
> but that's life,' " he says. "They weren't taught how to
> save the environment when they were growing up."
> (Better 1992)

Despite occasional references to schooling, children's environmental awareness is often portrayed as "natural," emerging from an essential and timeless quality of childhood.

> Kids are ... more instinctively tied in, more connected
> [to environmental issues]. (Slesin 1991)

> [Kids] see things in black or white. You either save the
> elephants or you don't, you either save the whales or you
> don't. Teachers, parents and environmentalists say this
> eco-enthusiasm is the product of children's natural inter-
> est in plants and animals.... Kids have such a natural
> empathy for the world.... They find it very easy to em-
> brace the idea that we should protect it. (Boccella 1991)

At the same time, children's ecological concerns are consistently ridiculed and trivialized, reduced to "pet peeves," "soap boxes," a caricature of "political correctness," and religious fundamentalism.

> Like many her age, Rachel has become a junior eco-evangelist. (Boccella 1991)

> Solomon is a member of YES—Youth for Environmental Sanity, a troupe of eco-crusaders that travels around the country preaching an evangelical mission. (Better 1992)

> Like an army of diminutive missionaries, many children are bringing home to their parents all kinds of messages about the way things are in the world—and the way things ought to be. (Garelik 1991)

Laced throughout the discourse on children's "ecovigilant-ism" is a subtext of irritation bordering on fear—children are presented as rigid and intolerant environmental police.

> If teenagers have been remarkably successful at forcing [environmental] concessions, it's probably because they have intransigence on their side. (Better 1992)

> Absolutely no plastic is an unwritten law in the household. "If something is in plastic, I have to hide if I want to use it," [a mother] said. (Slesin 1991)

> [Children] learn that these things are objectively wrong, at a time when they're too young to have learned a measure of empathy and understanding to shade the primary colors of censure. We try to tell them it's not polite to make a citizen's arrest at the bus stop because someone is puffing away [on a cigarette]. (Quindlen 1990)

> Kids tend to be very dictatorial and insistent anyway. They feel that there's a right way to do something. It's

like when kids used to tell their parents to stop smoking.
Now they are insistent that they do everything that's
environmentally correct. (Boccella 1991)

Rhetoric describing children's environmental political action
as "confrontational" or "guerrilla tactics" reverses former constructions of children as "overburdened" by adult concerns, in
language that is at once condescending and critical: "Kids are
leaning on their elders to kick bad habits, be kind to animals and
help save the planet. Talk about parent guilt!" (Garelik 1991).
The environmental actions children are said to demand are
couched almost exclusively in terms of personal, private deci-
sions about "changing behaviors"—turning off the faucet, recycling plastic bottles, reusing brown-paper bags. When broader
social action is mentioned, it usually concerns consumer
behavior—boycotting products that are harmful to the atmosphere, for example, or buying only products that have a mini-
mum of packaging.
Upon closer investigation there is little difference between
conservative discourses of children as environmental political
pawns and liberal discourses of children as ecotyrants and parental nightmares. The hinge that brings the two together is concern, not exclusively or even primarily for children, but rather
for consumption.
Conservatives see environmental activism as a political threat
to unregulated commerce and ever-increasing consumer mar-
kets. And they (rightly) see children actively embracing environmentalism as their issue. Without a touch of irony or conscience,
conservative discourse decries the use of children by environmentalists and then proceeds to exploit images of them as political pawns—empty vessels being filled with environmental
propaganda—in a blatant attempt to counteract environmentalist trends they so rightly fear.
Liberals, on the other hand, are much less straightforward in
their politics and portrayals of children. They depict children
as innocent victims of environmental disaster and also de-
monize them as ecotyrants and environmental vigilantes. Not
surprisingly, liberal discourse wants it both ways. Liberal-
environmental rhetoric expresses care and concern for children's emotional well-being and fear and loathing for ecosmart

"little darlings" eagerly packed off to summer camp. Children are encouraged to be aware of global environmental problems, are provided with simple lifestyle solutions, and then are roundly criticized for demanding the most minor of changes in patterns of family consumption.

The paradoxical attempt to both promote and contain children's environmental activism is framed in imagery that at once elevates and demonizes environmentally active children, and ultimately views them as a potential political threat. However, contradictions within both liberal and conservative discourse point, not only to the incorporation and co-optation of children's environmental concern, but also to the possibility of real social change engendered in the environmental debate. Children, it seems, are aware of this process and possibility. Responding to a typically ambivalent article in *The New York Times Magazine* on "Green Teens," a sixteen-year-old girl writes: "I would hope that in the future my own parents and older people in general would see that what we young people are fighting for it not a joke. As a 'green teen' I have learned that recycling is not enough. . . . Without the 'green teen' of today, the earth will be a shambles tomorrow" (*New York Times Magazine* 1992).

Children know that they are presented in contradictory and often belittling ways in all manner of environmentalist rhetoric. But distorted images of themselves are not the only contradictions children confront in popular messages about environmental crisis, as becomes apparent in the "selling" of environmental crisis to kids.

2

■

Selling
Environmentalism
to Kids

He who dies with the most toys wins.
—Bumper sticker on an undergraduate's Toyota

Environmental-crisis messages targeting children pervade every realm of child life. Department stores display all manner of children's clothing—down to diapers—sporting brightly colored planets, rainforests, wildlife, and slogans, with colorful tags that read Kids Talk—Save Our Earth, Enviro Team, and Keep Our World Clean. Cereal boxes are decorated with endangered animal species, fish sticks packages contain "Clean Ocean Kids" activity books, animal cracker boxes admonish children to "Help Save the Animals." Burger King bags depict a burger in the shape of the planet and brag about their "new earth happy packaging" in the handwriting of a child:

> You will probably notice that our sandwiches now come in paper wrapping instead of a box. That's because we figured the world could probably use *15,000* less tons of trash a year. And less trash means less trucks to carry it. Which means less gas, and a lot less air pollution. Not to mention the reduction in packaging the packaging has to be shipped in! All in all, its just one of the ways we are trying to make the world a nicer place to eat.

Not only are children targets of "green" advertising campaigns; innumerable books, magazines, cartoons, commercials, television shows, movies, videos, and other products of popular culture are explicitly designed to arouse children's environmental concern. Barney and *Sesame Street, Mister Rogers* and Nickelodeon, MTV and VH-1 all devote a significant portion of their children's television programming to environmental issues. There is an "earth-based" environmental magazine for kids, an environmental cartoon called *Captain Planet and the Planeteers,* and a seemingly limitless supply of books telling children "how to save the earth." From the time they have their endangered-animal breakfast cereal in the morning until they climb into their "save-the-rainforest" pajamas at night, children eat and sleep, read and watch TV about environmental crisis.

Often it is difficult to decipher what adults want children to do about environmental crisis. Are children supposed to curtail their consumption and conserve "natural resources?" or buy the latest Toxic Crusader or Captain Planet doll? Are they innocent victims of imminent global disaster? or tyrannical "ecoterrorists" cowing their parents into recycling the trash? And when they are taught about the ecological hazards of strip mining, forest clearcutting, driftnet fishing, toxic-waste dumping, oil spills, nuclear-waste storage, overcrowded landfills, ozone depletion, the greenhouse effect, the effects of pesticides, ad infinitum . . . what exactly are kids supposed to *do?*

In this chapter I analyze "green" products of the popular culture, and in particular the environmental cartoon, *Captain Planet and the Planeteers,* to decipher messages being transmitted to children in the name of "saving the planet." I argue that these popular media and their save-the-planet messages epitomize a *liberal-environmental paradox;* an ideology that seeks at once to protect the "ecosystem" and to preserve the social status quo. Trying to "save the planet" *and* maintain social relations in their present form is a contradiction; an impossible and politically disempowering task. It is also an extremely popular idea and cause, especially among the affluent white middle class.

A Trip to the Local Library

It is an excruciatingly hot and humid Thursday afternoon, normal summer weather for the southeastern United States, too hot even to enjoy sunbathing at the sandy beach or body-surfing in the salty Atlantic waves. Instead we are driving to seek darker sanctuary in the cool relief of the air-conditioned public library. I want to look again at a book I first heard read to third-graders two years ago in an upstate New York classroom. *Only a Dream,* I think it is called, or something like that—a morality tale about a boy who has a series of bad dreams after he throws a piece of litter on the ground. The computer in the children's room at the library cannot locate a book by that title, so I ask the librarian, a cheerful woman named Samantha, who immediately knows which book I mean. *"Just* a Dream," she smiles knowingly. "I'm not sure it's in. It's a popular one." As we walk together through the waist-high stacks, she steers me to the shelves of environmental books for kids. Luckily, the book is in, and I check it out for three weeks, along with an armload of various other "ecobooks" designed for children. There are no fewer than thirty-three such books in this library's collection, listed in a green-paper pamphlet prepared by the children's librarian, with titles like *My First Green Book, Earth Keepers, Recycle!,* and *Going Green.* By a chance oversight, *50 Simple Things Kids Can Do to Save the Earth* is not on the list. When I inquire, I am told the library has the book but it is almost always checked out, as is the case today.

Green Reading and Viewing

Just a Dream

Environmental books designed for children come in two basic genres: the middle-class morality tale and simple solutions for saving the planet. The 1990 book *Just a Dream,* by Chris Van Allsburg, is a classic example of the former. A cautionary tale with an environmental moral, *Just a Dream* is the story of a boy who thoughtlessly tosses a waxed-paper doughnut wrapper on the ground and lives to regret the dire consequences of this wanton act of ecological destruction. Opening with an epigraph from the Pogo comic strip, "We have met the enemy and he is us," Van Allsburg uses large color illustrations to draw us into an insular and private world of middle-class affluence, one that is destined to be disrupted and devastated by the isolated actions of a boy who looks to be no more than eight years old. Walter's crimes (besides being a bona fide litterer, he also prefers watching television to sorting the family's trash, and he thinks it is silly to get a tree sapling for a birthday present) take place in the context of a beautifully rendered suburban environment, where all the houses are two stories tall, spacious, and freshly painted, and the lawns are lush green and newly mowed.

The plot is a takeoff on *A Christmas Carol,* with an environmental twist. Walter throws down his trash, fantasizes about a fun, technological future after watching a television show, and then falls asleep, only to be subjected to a series of nightmares wherein his bed acts as a magic-carpet ride into an unforgiving future of ecological peril. Toasters and toilets and big bags of garbage bury his neighborhood in a mountain of trash. Snowy Mount Everest is a huge hotel resort, and the Grand Canyon is so smoggy you can see it only by buying color postcards. Smokestacks and automobiles choke streets and sky, and ducks fly wearily in futile search of a lost pond. When Walter is at last released from his tormented sleep he realizes (surprise!) robots and little airplanes of the future are not important. What really matters is that he run as fast as his little bare feet can carry him to go *pick up that jelly doughnut bag* and *sort all that trash!* When Walter plants the tree sapling he now wants for his birthday, he is rewarded that night with a pastoral dream: his middle-class neighborhood now has mature trees. The future secure, but for the bigger trees everything remains exactly the same.

The Lorax

Almost twenty years prior to the publication of *Just a Dream,* another environmental tale with a quite different moral made its appearance in the popular children's literature. Although Dr. Suess's story of the Lorax also enlists children's environmental concern, it focuses, not on the isolated acts of an individual *child,* but on a capitalist ethos embodied in the form of a (somewhat) now penitent Once-ler. In *Just a Dream* Walter is temporarily punished for messing around with middle-class mores against littering but is immediately redeemed; everything is the same—the neighborhood, the yard, only better with bigger trees—the moment he cleans up his act. In *The Lorax* the consequences of environmental destruction are long-lasting, perhaps final, unless . . . "UNLESS someone like you cares a whole awful lot, nothing's going to get better. It's not." What were children asked to care about almost a quarter of a century ago in *The Lorax?* The dank, smelly darkness at the far end of town where the Gricklegrass grows didn't get that way because some kid dropped his doughnut bag. Suess is quite clear on who devastated *this* town and drove the old Lorax away. And the Once-ler himself will tell how it happened "if you are willing to pay." For of course it is the Once-ler who came to this town with his head full of dreams about truffula trees. Trees that nourished all who lived in the land plowed down with a chop for the Once-ler's new shop. And despite all the warnings the crabby old Lorax could give, the Once-ler keeps "biggering" his business of making silly thneeds, "a Fine-Something-That-All-People-Need!"

Whereas Van Allsburg uses notalgic images of pastoral neighborhoods to draw us into a insular and private world, Suess uses snappy dialogue and witty caricature to juxtapose several social actors: the "fast-track" adult Once-ler entrepreneur, the grumpy old Lorax who speaks for the trees, the boychild witness to history and bearer of the last seed. And, most important, the environmental villain in *The Lorax* is not children but corporate greed and "manufactured" needs.

This simple moral was more common in the 1970s around the time *The Lorax* appeared. Then, even the United Nations recognized the dual danger to democracy and the environment that unregulated transnational corporations (TNCs) pose in a global economy, as it sought to hammer out an international code of conduct to monitor the actions of TNCs. Two decades later, multinational corporations acting as virtual "stateless nations" control economies and governments; hold developing countries hostage with the threat of capital flight; and invoke an ideology of "free trade" to avoid public accountability, repress labor organizing, and ignore environmental regulation (Bleifuss 1994).

Such corporate behavior remains the norm and in fact is rapidly worsening, but geopolitics and populist concern about rampant corporate capitalism have changed significantly since the early days of environmentalism and the first official Earth Day. With the widely celebrated "collapse of communism" in the Soviet Union and Eastern Europe, market capitalism marches onto global hegemony, "popular heroes of our times are money-makers, speculators . . . the 'winners' as opposed to the 'losers' " (Singer 1994:124), and socialist principles are effectively discredited. As both symptom and symbol of this ideological shift, the United Nations' Code of Conduct on Transnational Corporations was dismantled without fanfare in 1992 and "died a quiet bureaucratic death" (Bleifuss 1994). It is specifically within this social and historical context that children today are being told with insistent regularity that it is *they* who are the culprits in environmental disaster.

Ferngully: The Last Rainforest

And if not children, then dark, amorphous, evil forces are often blamed for ecological destruction. We can see this theme at work in *Ferngully: The Last Rainforest. Ferngully* opened in movie theatres in 1992, riding the twin waves of the twentieth anniversary of Earth Day and the huge success of the 1989 Disney animated "classic" *The Little Mermaid.* Here gender enters into the environmental configuration with the main protagonist portrayed as a highly sexualized little fairy named Chrysta, who (predictably) falls for a big hunk of a human named Zak. Magie, a toothless old green-eyed witch manages to contain Hexus, the dark, evil, amorphous force of environmental destruction, inside a big, gnarled tree in the middle of the rainforest. "Everything on earth is a balance between the forces of destruction and the magic force of creation," Magie tells her flighty protégée Chrysta. "There is not a force in nature that could release Hexus." But man, wielding the unnatural force of random and wanton technology, lays waste to Magie's work and releases the evil Hexus from his gnarly prison.

In *Ferngully* corporate greed is depersonalized and *naturalized.* Workers operating the vicious tree "leveler" while clear-cutting the rainforest are depicted as fat, uncouth, working-class slobs who stuff their faces and talk "like dis" with mouths full of food; stupid victims of their own insatiable need for immediate gratification. However, no corporations are shown providing the capital for this rainforest logging venture, not even a representative of what surely must be a massive multinational undertaking. Neither is any explanation given for *why* the rainforest is being leveled in the first place. Evil is presented as always and everywhere a part of *nature,* released in its latest incarnation by technology but a natural force of destruction and thus invincible, inevitable, except for the magic power of creation.

As in *The Lorax* hope is held in a seed of life, passed from Magie to Chrysta, who plants it in the belly of the beast. The metaphor of "the seed" is common in environmental rhetoric, a symbol of life, potential, and hope. Less known is the role the seed plays in patriarchal discourse. Notions of the seed as containing the essence of "life" reinforce social relations in which paternity is the defining relationship and "impregnated" women are reduced to the status of potted plants. A matrilineal reversal of roles seemingly takes place in *Ferngully* when Chrysta "impregnates" the evil (male) Hexus with a magic seed passed to her by her "mother/mentor," the good witch Magie. But as Barbara Katz Rothman notes in another context, maintaining the centrality of "the seed" incorporates women into a patriarchal ideology that reduces social kinship relationships "to property rights" based on genetics (1989:36).

The "magic power of creation" theme offers easy, simple, and decidedly unpolitical solutions to environmental problems. Unlike *The Lorax* and more like *Just a Dream,* redemption in *Ferngully* comes instantly and effortlessly with the assistance of magic forces. In *Just a Dream* it is nocturnal time travel, in *Ferngully* it is fairy dust and magic seeds, and in *Captain Planet and the Planeteers* it is five magic rings. But magic is not the only thing being sold to kids in popular discourse about environmental crisis.

Global Visions and the Liberal-Environmental Paradox: *Captain Planet and the Planeteers*

Watching Captain Planet

The theatrical (and pedagogical) premise of *Captain Planet and the Planeteers* is succinctly provided in its public-relations kit:

> Gaia, the spirit of the Earth, awakens from a 100-year nap to discover the devastating effects people have had on our planet's environment in the 20th century. Fearing for the future, she calls upon five special young people from around the world—Wheeler (North America), Linka (Soviet Union), Gi (Asia), Kwame (Africa) and Ma-Ti (South America)—to lead the battle against further destruction of the Earth. She gives these planeteers magic rings that enable each of them to control one element of nature—Earth, Fire, Water, Wind and a very special power, Heart. When the planeteers join their powers together, Captain Planet, an environmental superhero, is summoned. Together, they battle the eco-villains who are trying to destroy the Earth.
>
> Each episode ends with a [thirty-second] epilogue including tips for viewers on how they can be a part of the environmental solution through recycling, carpooling, etc. (TBS 1990)

Ritually reprised before every episode of *Captain Planet,* this basic premise (minus mention of the thirty-second tag) is immediately followed by several minutes of aggressively loud and fast-paced commercial advertisements selling junk food, toys, paraphernalia, and other television shows to kids. Typically, the cartoon returns to some dastardly deed being perpetrated against the earth by one or more often comic and entertaining ecovillains.

In an episode aired in the fall of 1992, Zarm, evil spirit of the earth, descends into a peaceful Third World–like village of generic indigenous people, armed with a "dream machine" that provides peasants with large automobiles, indoor plumbing, central air conditioning, and other consumable objects of the First World. This might represent the redistribution of technology and goods to peoples historically not only denied such goods but exploited for their natural resources and human labor to produce them for others. Not surprisingly, this is not the tack producers of *Captain Planet* take in their plot. Rather, there unfolds a cautionary tale in which greed, aggression, and pollution quite naturally follow any attempts at economic advancement in developing nations. By the end of the show peasants are shown willingly rejecting progress and technology and returning gratefully to primordial poverty.

Meanwhile, with unremitting regularity, two- or three-minute blocks of commercial advertisements are interspersed throughout every *Captain Planet* narrative, framing it and providing its deeper structure. Always depicted as comfortably housed and stylishly dressed, children of the West can be seen driving big, convertible cars while eating Apple Jacks, riding rocket-powered tubes of toothpaste through outer space, having their hands "controlled" by uncontrollable urges to eat Chips Ahoy cookies, and so on. When the thirty-second tag finally arrives, admonishing children to turn off the lights and tune-up the car, it is framed by advertisements, two minutes preceding the tag and four minutes following the closing credits.

A logic that argues it is right for us to own cars but others carts, in which children are encouraged on the one hand to conserve and on the other to purchase Barbie's latest dream house, is clearly paradoxical. But it is a paradox that serves a practical and pedagogic function.

Selling Captain Planet

Captain Planet and the Planeteers made its television debut on September 15, 1990, as "the world's first animated environmental action-adventure program" (TBS 1990). Brainchild of Ted Turner, board chairman and president of Turner Broadcasting System, and a joint venture of TBS and DIC Enterprises (a major production company specializing in children's programming), the "enviro-tainment" cartoon airs on more than 220 network affiliate and independent stations nationwide, can be found on cable television on TBS, and is shown in over fifty countries covering almost every continent, creating a vast global market.

Not only is "the world's first environmental superhero" on Saturday and Sunday mornings as a cartoon show, Captain Planet is also "a whole line of fun-filled and imaginative products" including "apparel (for Planeteers of all ages), video games, school supplies, shoes, Halloween costumes, slumber bags and tents, lunch boxes, sports bottles and stickers" (TBS 1990). Even a recent Tupperware ® catalog has Captain Planet appearing as a reusable plastic lunch kit and tumbler set for "earth-smart kids!" Just after making its pitch for kids to buy Tupperware ® products, and then for kids to fight pollution, the Tupperware ad concludes with a pitch for kids to "watch the number-one rated Captain Planet show. . . . See your local listings for times and channels."

The merger being forged here, quite apparent and unabashed, blends entertainment and education, prosocial and procommercial, and describes the current liberal paradox in environmentalizing kids: at the same time that they are admonished to conserve, recycle, reuse, and respect the limits of the earth, children are aggressively canvassed and cajoled to buy products and consume goods.

Turner Broadcasting System's own expensive, glossy, and conspicuously "printed on recycled paper" public-relations packet is quite forthcoming in acknowledging its product-marketing strategy ("Licensing and Merchandising: A Cooperative Effort," TBS 1990). The company follows a now firmly entrenched practice of creating licensed character products that precede and then drive their subsequent cartoons with the express purpose of selling merchandise to kids. While historically cartoons and cartoon characters were created as entertainment and then often licensed out to merchandisers and advertisers for commercial use, today (as the TBS package makes explicit), the licensing and merchandising of cartoon characters is not only an integral aspect of cartoon production but more often than not its raison d'être.

Tom Engelhardt (1987) attributes this crass commercialism in children's television production to deregulation of the industry by Ronald Reagan in 1983, when policy guidelines for children's shows and limits on advertising time were rescinded. One consequence, the program-length commercial cartoon, has premise, planning, and production that revolve entirely around the licensing and marketing of character products generated for sale. He-Man, Strawberry Shortcake, the Smurfs, the Transformers, Care Bears, Teenage Mutant Ninja Turtles all represent calculated "made-for-TV" market strategies designed for the promotion and sale of "lovable" or "action-adventure" protagonists.

Even the 1990 Children's Television Act—which once again mandates limits on advertising time, requires stations to air educational and informational shows for children, and specifically bans children's programs that are designed to plug products—has not reversed this trend (Center for Media Education 1992).

> While broadcasters are required by law to document the value of their programming for children, many are not reporting adequately to the Federal Communications Commission, and many of those broadcasters that do report are touting such diverse shows as *GI Joe, Leave It to Beaver,* and *Santa Claus Is Coming to Town* as "prosocial," educational, and/or informational for children. (Aufderheide 1992)

Enter Ted Turner with a new idea for a children's cartoon—*Captain Planet and the Planeteers*—selling not only product licenses and action figurines but a full-fledged "global environmental ethic" (TBS 1990). This merger of corporate mass-marketing practices and environmental pedagogy represents, I believe, an essentially flawed project and epitomizes a paradox in liberal environmentalism.

Managing the Planet

> *We have to manage our planet, and we have to do it on a global basis. It's the greatest challenge that humanity has ever faced, and it's the most exciting time to be alive.* R. E. Turner (TBS 1990, emphasis in original)

Ted Turner presents the notion of managing the planet as a thrilling and unprecedented challenge. Others have been inclined to cast a more wary eye toward global management as at best threatening democratic participation and at worst promoting totalitarian responses (see Bookchin 1990; Barber 1992). Critics of the General Agreement on Trade and Tariffs (GATT) fear that a slide toward antidemocracy has already begun, citing recently enacted provisions that give a secret GATT governing body the power to overrule any national or local environmental legislation deemed "unnecessarily" obstructive to trade (see Citizen Trade Watch Campaign 1992; Dawkins 1992; Rosenthal 1992; U.S. Environmental and Consumer Groups 1992; Wiener 1992).[1]

Global management refers to multinational corporate practices, with the "globe" reduced to a site of flexible capital and flexible labor. Integral as well to liberal environmental notions of "managing the planet" is the presentation of nature as, alternately, mother and resource. She/it must be protected so that "we" (postindustrial, late-capitalist, consumerist nations) can sustain our preferred standard of living.[2] Just as women in labor are "managed" by physicians who, operating under patriarchal notions of "protection" and control, reduce a birthing woman's activity and experience to the status of a manipulable object—"labor" (Rothman 1993), so is nature as mother and resource objectified and dominated in the name of "care."

Ethical concerns, such as responsibility for future generations or for the quality of the biosphere, are frequently espoused in liberal-environmental discourse. These concerns, however, are always conflated with the unarticulated, hegemonic assumption that (responsible) capitalism, (liberal) patriarchy, and (benevolent) racism are inevitable natural facts. Meanwhile, analysis of the inherent drive within capitalism to both devour global environmental resources and to reproduce egregious social injustice is invisible in global-management schemes and absent in liberal-environmentalist ideology.[3] Therein lies the paradox; for while the desire to "save the planet" may be experienced as sincere by its proponents, liberal environmentalism is fatally undermined at the outset by its contradictory call for simultaneous environmental change and political, economic, and social reproduction.

The Making of an Environmental Superhero

"I had a mandate from Ted to create a superhero, to make a cartoon called Captain Planet." This was reported to me by a woman who, as a high-level producer of *Captain Planet and the Planeteers,* is responsible in large measure for its creative direction and environmental content. I cite her frequently throughout the remainder of this chapter. All of her quotes are taken from an interview I conducted with her over the telephone in the summer of 1992. The *Captain Planet* public relations kit describes the conception of the cartoon in a similar way: "In the fall of 1988, TBS Board Chairman and President R.E. Turner had an idea for an environmental superhero. 'The champion of environmental causes should be a superhero who sets out to battle environmental problems in order to preserve the Earth's natural resources,' he said. 'He will be *Captain Planet*' " (TBS 1990).

Turner's mandate for a male superhero named "Captain Planet" to protect "resources" is immediately telling in many of its ideological assumptions. The earth is portrayed as a passive repository (a resource) in need of a (male) superhero to preserve (and subsequently exploit) its treasures, by force of military authority (*Captain* Planet) if necessary. Almost by definition a liberal-environmental agenda will at the same time attempt to be politically correct: " 'We wanted to create a superhero who would not be representative of one country,' explains Turner. 'He had to be someone that every kid could look up to.' With that in mind, the team began developing 'the look' for its superhero" (TBS 1990).

Just as in media-driven contemporary politics, where "the look" is considered crucial for popular success, so it goes in cartoon marketing. Yet within the politics of representation, where issues of class, gender, race, sexual orientation, able-bodiedness, and anticolonialism create a complex and treacherous terrain for liberal image-packaging, Captain Planet is clearly *not* a superhero "every kid" can look up to, despite the careful attempt to create a "universal" appeal: "Captain Planet was the most difficult of the characters to conceptualize. We knew we had to make him universal, so we made him out of crystal, and gave him the colors of life: sky-blue skin, grass-green hair and earthy brown eyes" (TBS 1990).

Take away the "natural" trappings, however, the blue tint and green hair, and what is revealed is a typical white, male super-hero, universal only within its own tautology (all superheroes are massively muscular and towering white men). Among his classic Nordic features—strong, square jaw; small, straight nose; thin upper lip and gleaming white smile—only Captain Planet's "earthy brown eyes" (conventionally for superheroes a steely cold blue) stand in stark contrast to what is otherwise an arche-typal, made-in-the-U.S.A. male god.

Children's Views of Captain Planet

For Engelhardt, children's television of the mideighties reflected a "self-portrait of the Reagan era," with "the Universe of the Action-Figure Superhero" representing the thrill of Star Wars military technology (1987:87). This is the era in which Captain Planet was conceived. Even his ritual departing cry, "The power is *yours!*" closely mimics Prince Adam's invocation "I have the power," uttered when transforming into He-Man. Institutional-ized and commercialized for well over a decade, male super-hero "masters of the universe" are common stock on children's television, and many children are savvy critics and consumers of such narrative (and plastic) figures.

Several of the children I interviewed relate positively to the superhero, Captain Planet, and they favorably view his job as "cleaning up the planet" and "taking care of the bad guys" who pollute. However, doubts about the ethics of depicting a super-hero taking care of environmental crisis did arise for some chil-dren. Eleven-year-old Jennifer, who lives in an environmentally active family, put it this way:

> I didn't think [*Captain Planet*] was good stuff to watch.... It was bizarre and it wasn't down to earth. I mean they were making stuff so, they were making it seem like only a superhero could do it. And you know, I don't think that's true because if they're saying that then they're saying that real people can't recycle. They're just

saying that super people can help save the planet and I,
that's why I didn't like it, I didn't think that was true.

While agreeing that environmental problems won't be solved
by superheroes, Benjamin, nine years old and also from an activist family, takes a more favorable view of Captain Planet's pedagogic role:

> It's mostly just . . . for your amusement. . . . I mean none
> of this could really happen in real life. . . . But it tells you
> about the problems on like the [planet]. I mean they
> could never be solved in the ways they solve it [in the
> cartoon]. Like [when] Captain Planet comes out and
> does all this [superhero stuff].

Benjamin contrasts the environmental superhero with that
hero's historical prototype, Superman, noting the effectiveness
of depicting Captain Planet as dependent on the powers of nature and vulnerable to environmental problems such as pollution and toxic waste.

> But it's not as if Captain Planet was Superman. 'Cause
> Captain Planet goes out and he gets hurt, and he gets his
> power drained, and they have to lift him up. . . . He just
> has the powers of the environment. He really can't like
> fire a laser at your head or anything. And he wouldn't. . . .
> He actually sounds like he's doing hard work. . . . And
> they make his hero character sort of vulnerable. . . . I
> wouldn't say that's his weakness; I'd say that was his
> strength. . . . That's why people sorta like him.

Captain Planet is an ambivalent narrative figure, a floating
signifier: standard superhero for some children, positive role
model for others, meaningless or even hazardous in other children's views. But what of the Planeteers? For as we all know,
every superhero needs his cast of supporting characters: "Turner wanted the series to appeal to children of all ages and races.
To that end, five Planeteers were created—each from a different
region of the globe and each with a different power. Turner's
idea grew into a series, *Captain Planet and the Planeteers*"
(TBS 1990). Thus are *children* brought into this configuration

of cartoon, crisis, and environmental superhero. "The idea origi-
nated by Ted Turner was basically to instill an ethic of international environmental cooperation in kids, and [to] show them
that by combining their powers they could create something
that's much greater than the parts, create a whole which is kind
of embodied in Captain Planet."[4]

Five Kids from Five Countries with Five Magic Powers

The Planeteers, carefully gender-, nation-, and color-coordinated,
are "special people" chosen to help save the planet, and each is
provided with a discrete elemental power. As such they constitute a veritable United Nations/Nature.

Wheeler, the U.S. planeteer, is white—but not Jewish, not
Italian, certainly not black, Korean, Latino, Caribbean—and
from Brooklyn. (This in itself approaches contradiction, given
the demographic characteristics of the culturally diverse New
York City borough.) But for his red hair, pinkish skin, and
slightly shorter stature, he is the spitting image of Captain Planet
himself. This brash and impulsive all-American planeteer—the
only one of the group to wear long pants—holds the power of
fire. Kwame, the only black planeteer, comes from Africa and
holds the power of earth, grounding the so-called Third World
in both a literal and figurative sense. He is portrayed as a calm
and sensible leader and is provided with a strong and muscular
body. By contrast, Ma-ti, the Latino planeteer, is quite short and
childlike. He holds the "very special" power of heart. "Heart"
might recall the excess emotionality stereotypically attributed
by people of the Northern Hemisphere to those of the Southern.
Here it appears to represent indigenous peoples not fully developed, a sweet, nonthreatening southern neighbor to balance the
impulsive and fiery neighbor to the north.

The young women Planeteers are of sturdy body and paramili-
tary style. Gi—whose features, body size, and hair style are
remarkably similar to Ma-ti's from the South—stands for a generalized "Asia." Her elemental power is water, and she communes
with dolphins and other such sea creatures. Except for a demon-

strated love of fish, little about Gi can be explicitly identified as Japanese; neither is Japan's global economic clout evident in the character's depiction or development. Linka, the former Soviet turned ambiguously "Eastern European," speaks with a bad Russian accent and holds the power of wind. She has a fondness for music, an analytical mind, and frequently plays the mature, if somewhat stiff, former Soviet foil to Wheeler's brash American adolescence. One senses a potential "melting of the Cold War" romantic subtext brewing between the two characters.

These then are Turner's multicultural Planeteers, his vision of international environmental cooperation. Standing in stark contrast to this liberal-environmental image-packaging are typical responses made by children about the Planeteers. Most children I interviewed recall the Planeteers as nameless holders of magic rings that "spurt out" magic powers and can conjure up Captain Planet. Robert, a six-year-old white boy from a financially struggling, single-parent family, provides a typical description of the Planeteers: "I don't know what they look like but they have rings to make Captain Planet combine: fire, water, wind . . ." Timothy, eleven, and from a white, upper-middle-class divorced family, gives a similar account of the Planeteers: "It's about . . . these four kids from different countries or something, or five . . . and they just like try to prevent stuff, and I think when the rings come together or something Captain Planet comes . . . against . . . bad guys that are ruining the environment."

Captain Planet is more salient for these children than are the Planeteers, who emerge almost uniformly as two-dimensional figures amplified and made interesting to children only through the power of their magic rings. Liberal environmentalism falters in its quest to foster a multinational eco-activist identity among children through the promotion of Planeteers. Here it seems to succeed best in instilling a powerful interest in magic rings.

Gaia: Negotiating the Terrain of Nature

Implicit in both patriarchal discourse and the liberal defense of capital is a deep ambivalence about the status of nature, as mother to be protected and as resource to be exploited.

The basic message [in *Captain Planet*] is to learn that
we are part of the earth, and that we have the responsibility to protect the earth.... As the thinking species we
have a responsibility to protect nature.... Nature's not
just a bunch of natural resources that have been put
here for us to use up as fast as possible.... We have to
change our perception of the way we view ourselves
and the ways of the planet, in relationship to the
planet.... We're part of it, it's not ours. And we have to
protect it because we depend on it for survival.[5]

The crux of any environmental ethic is respect for nature. But
beyond this basic premise lie many different interpretations of
how, why, and what constitutes "nature" and "respect." Conflicting notions of human and nature relations are demonstrated in
the executive producer's statement: On the one hand we humans are urged to "change our perceptions" so as to see ourselves as part of nature, and nature as inherently worthwhile,
"not just a bunch of natural resources." But inextricably intertwined with this potentially subversive and egalitarian view of
nature is the simultaneous notion of hierarchy and exploitation:
we as "the thinking species" are urged to "protect nature because we depend on it for [our] survival."

Whereas Captain Planet the superhero was brainchild of Ted
Turner, Gaia, spirit of the earth, was created by a woman, the
cartoon's original executive producer, to balance a perceived
slant toward boys and "male energy:" "I put Gaia in to balance
Captain Planet... to balance the energy, the male and female
energy." As a cartoon character, Gaia is supposed to reflect the
notion of nature as nurturant and feminine; taken at face value
this is a problematic correlation. Some feminists argue that asso-
ciating women with nature (as opposed to culture) is always a
bad idea and ultimately a patriarchal tool for denigrating and
oppressing both women and nature (see de Beauvoir 1952;
Firestone 1970; Ortner 1974; Williamson 1986:213–21; Seager
1993:11). Other feminists of various theoretical and political
persuasions disagree, arguing that within the conventional trope
woman/nature lies a potentially subversive message: so-called
natural, womanly qualities such as compassion, nurturance, and
empathy are invaluable *learned* capacities that preclude exploi-

tation and oppression and are thus crucial for promoting social justice and the survival of the planet (see Rothman 1989; Ruddick 1989; Diamond and Orenstein 1990; Y. King 1990).

Although visually rendering Gaia much like a Barbie doll, albeit with dark brown hair and a deep tan, her mother/creator demonstrates a budding awareness of this character's potential subversiveness: "Gaia is a very special character. . . . She is the embodiment of the planet itself. She is compassionate towards all living things and feels the pain of the Earth's destruction" (TBS 1990). However, this subversive potential is never developed in the cartoon narratives. The "spirit of the earth" remains a secondary character, and the children I interviewed show a remarkable lack of interest in the Gaia figure. Only one child spontaneously mentions the character by name and role. When Gaia is recalled, it is vaguely as "the lady who gives out the rings." One child, a six-year-old girl, remembers her as "the girl-lady that can fly off in the air. . . . She didn't have to have a ring on . . . 'cause she's one, well I think she's Captain Planet's mother or something, or a friend." More often, even when probed, children had no recall of "a lady" on the cartoon aside from perhaps a "girl" Planeteer or an occasional female guest character. While one might expect children to anthropomorphize nature and thus perhaps view "it" as "her" fairly readily, most children I interviewed paid scant attention to the Gaia character, rarely recalling her or mentioning her by name.

"It's Everyone's Fault; It's Nobody's Real Fault"

When I talked to Max, ten years old and from a white middle-class, two-parent family, he reflected on *Captain Planet* and universal responsibility for the environment:

It's everyone. Everyone does something not good for the environment. It's nobody's real fault. Like, when I was little, I watched that *Captain Planet,* and . . . there's like this bad guy and the good guy. And I guess, we're the bad guys and there's not going to be like a miracle or anything. It's up to us though to prevent it [environmental destruction.] ... There's no Captain Planet going to clean up the earth and make it beautiful again. It's up to us. We can't ... you know, we're the bad guys and we have to turn into good guys, I guess.

Max's thoughtful critique of *Captain Planet* demonstrates the degree to which liberal environmentalism demands that all of us accept personal responsibility for global environmental problems. Children in my study were particularly prone to this individualistic ideology, at least on a rhetorical level.

While the plot of *Captain Planet* always points to evil polluters with names like Hoggish Greedly or Doctor Blight, the message about environmental problems is a conflicting one, with superheroes and bad guys at the one end, and thirty-second proenvironmental tags urging kids to turn off the lights at the other. The producers of *Captain Planet and the Planeteers* see this formula as both entertaining and educating children about environmental problems.

> If we'd had a program like *Captain Planet* thirty years ago we wouldn't be in the mess we're in now ... Children are going to be, are the leaders of tomorrow. And because the issues are very complex ... they don't understand the issues. I mean you can't find one adult in a hundred thousand that can tell you what creates the ozone hole, or what causes global warming.... [After watching *Captain Planet*] they'll know what the ozone hole is, they'll know what [the] rainforest is, they'll know what acid rain is, they'll know what strip mining is, they'll know what driftnet fishing is.

And what are children supposed to *do* about these huge *corporate* problems?

> Well the kids that I've met feel really empowered ... [be]cause at the end [of the cartoon] they are told what they can do, you know. We give them a thirty-second tag.

Once again we confront the liberal environmental paradox: children are taught about huge, complex, institutional problems and are provided with simple and relatively painless individualistic solutions.

> I can tell you what I've seen ... children not letting their dads take bags out of the grocery store ... children starting little clean-up campaigns in their neighborhoods, starting recycling programs in their schools. A very funny example about a year and a half ago was when one of the grandchildren of one of our executives in the company, a little three year old, wasn't letting his daddy cut down a tree to build a carpark. ... And I think his daddy says, "Why not?" And the little boy says, "Because Captain Planet says trees are our friends."

Thus is the liberal environmental ethic complete. Trees are to be preserved in suburban backyards, and personal consumption is to be carefully monitored.

> So basically it becomes a new environmental ethic, it becomes part of normal behavior, not, not consuming. ... I mean it was consume, consume, consume.

Meanwhile, multinational corporations are essentially let off the hook. Business—far from being labeled a villain or, at the very least, in need of careful regulation—is heralded as "doing its share," of its "own free will," in the great universal push for a cleaner environment.

> We've gotten criticism from the ultra-right wing that we're anti-business, and we refute that by saying we are pro-responsible business. ... Business is changing of their own free will ... they're reducing packaging ... they're doing life cycle analysis on their products to make them less environmentally damaging, from top to tail, from the pollution it creates when it's manufactured to the amount of landfill space it takes up when it gets thrown away. ... Procter Gamble's been doing great strides. ... We're not twisting anybody's arms here. I mean it's terrific some of the things that are going on, very encouraging!

But the mess the planet is dealing with now—who is responsible for the degradation and waste? According to the liberal-environmental ethic, it is ignorance, not greed, that generated the crisis.

> You know, the people who have made the greatest mistakes on this planet, they have not been done out of... you know some of them have been done out of, out of greed, but most of them have been done out of ignorance.... People forty or fifty years ago really considered the ocean as a great big dumping ground. They didn't realize that we were killing off all the sea life, they truly didn't realize.

This producer reveals more than simple grammatical awkwardness when she shifts her emphasis from those most responsible for environmental disaster to the more abstract "mistakes." "The people who made the greatest mistakes" remain faceless and nameless. Responsibility is conveniently diffused. Corporate interests shielded yet again.

Consuming Environmental Culture

Environmental messages to children such as those typified in *Just a Dream, Ferngully,* and *Captain Planet and the Planeteers* graphically demonstrate a liberal misdirection of children's very real willingness to help save the planet. Through a contradictory promotion of conservation and consumption, and by exposing children to huge, complex, and corporately created environmental problems but providing them with only simplistic and individualistic solutions, liberal-environmental discourse provides salve but little substance for effectively directing children's environmental concern. Intertwining ideologies of patriarchy and militarism, capitalism and racism remain essentially intact in liberal environmentalism, undermining the promise of an activism that demands change not only in middle-class lifestyles and relations with nature but also and especially in oppressive social relations at the core of environmental crisis.

While ostensibly children's project is to "save the earth," what is most often promoted in popular environmental media are middle-class morals: keep your lawn clean, sort out the trash, plant a tree in your backyard, buy "environmentally friendly" products. Environmental problems are monumental and political, but the tasks for "solving" them are simple and individual. There is an emphasis on guilt in environmental messages to children along with a diffusion of responsibility promoting the notion of environmental crisis as everyone's and no one's "real" fault. With the problem of power and privilege eluded, environmentalism is reduced to a conflict-free politics. As Rosalind Coward notes:

> This absence of conflict is probably another reason why there has been far more approval for spreading the environmental message to children than there ever was for spreading the anti-racist and anti-sexist message. Teaching tolerance for different domestic arrangements is obviously considered far more dangerous than pressuring schools into creating wildlife gardens or introducing recycling themes. (1990:41)

Environmentalism becomes "largely a question of personal ethics or consumer choice" (1990:41). But while it is clear that the liberal-environmental message is flawed, an important question remains unanswered: How are children *responding* to the systematic calls they are getting to help save the planet?

Arguing that cultural productions such as *Captain Planet and the Planeteers* serve as more than simply entertaining or educational children's fare raises questions about the social function of culture. Whether or not children's consumer culture is progressive or oppressive, a site of resistance or co-optation, is a subject of debate among communication researchers specializing in children's media. Stephen Kline (1993), for example, supports Engelhardt in his condemnation of new marketing strategies that use children's cartoons as vehicles for selling promotional "character toys." Kline argues that while market-driven "culture industries" may deliver "what children want," those products may not be "good for [children] or for society in the long run." Children's fantasy worlds are being circumscribed and limited, says Kline, by contemporary "technicians of the imagination," whose trite narratives, stylized character development, and banal cultural products restrict children's socio-emotional development to a narrow and stereotypical range (1993:277–331).

Taking a different stand, Ellen Seiter (1993) argues that critics forget that children are actively *engaged* when they consume popular fare. Seiter takes both Kline and Engelhardt to task for ignoring complex gender issues that arise in "simplistic" cartoons for children. She argues that "licensed character shows were not essentially different from other animated programs for children that had been around since the 1960s: what was new about them was that it was girls—and very young girls at that—who were being approached as a separate audience" (1993:152–53). Both girls and boys are making real and meaningful choices in identification, says Seiter, within the limited sources of power and fantasy available to them in commercial culture (171). Children's consumer culture involves a "rebellion" that "may convey a resistance to parental [bourgeois] culture" (233). While carefully disclaiming television as a social and political cure-all ("Television viewing to the exclusion of other activities is debilitating and self-destructive in the long run if it leaves no time for the acquisition of skills that the *public* sphere will require" [234]), Seiter argues that television and children's commercial culture provide children with a wider view of the world, particularly those children who *lack* material resources (229).

Environmental themes directed at children are virtually ignored by Kline and are mentioned only in passing by Seiter, who notes that "the vaguely environmentalist themes that emerge in cartoons are usually inoffensive to parents, prosocial and relatively non-violent" (1993:159). While discussing gender difference in themes of "saving the world from toxicity" (cartoons aimed at boys employ the traditional plot of "direct battle with a villain using a weapon," while girls are motivated "as a group to act together as a team" [159]), Seiter's analysis ignores the meanings and significance that environmental-crisis themes hold both for the adults producing them and the children receiving and interpreting them. In this regard Coward raises an important point, arguing:

It would be very easy for children to be put off by the patronizing moralism which is often directed at them [in environmental media], were it not for the fact that almost all these products, books and programmes encourage children to "shame" adults, to pressurize adults about their consumerist lifestyle. What is clearly being recognised or offered here is the child's right to be not only represented but *powerful* within the family, even if largely in terms of consumer choices.... There is an important sense in which children are being encouraged to feel effective within their immediate environment. More significantly, they are being encouraged to be knowledgeable.... It remains to be seen whether adults will be able to resist using children as a moral dumping ground and equip them with [the] broader knowledge that the [environmental crisis] situation requires. (1990:41)

What kinds of knowledge are children getting from popular discourse about the environmental crisis? What is the meaning of environmental "empowerment" for children? Ultimately we return to the unanswered question: What do *children* make of all this environmental discourse? To better understand how children are understanding and embracing messages telling them to "save the planet," I turn next to children's drawings.

3
■

Children's Concerns about the Planet
Messages in Their Drawings

First save the planet, then you can watch cartoons.
—Slogan on an infant's T-shirt

Notions of Children's Environmental Concern

When Victoria watches sea lions being clubbed to death by trappers on a Discovery Channel nature show, what does she feel? When eight-year-old Jamal is told in his third-grade classroom that there are "too many people" in the world, especially in Africa and Asia, what does he think? When six-year-old Carolyn hears herself referred to as "Little Miss Ecology" by her father, what does it mean to her? When children learn about global warming or toxic-waste dumping on a *Captain Planet* cartoon and then hear Captain Planet say, "The power is yours!" what kind of power do they experience? How are children responding to bombardment by cultural messages telling them *they* have to save the planet?

Many adults imagine that messages about environmental crisis go right over the heads of little children. They assume that environmental issues are too abstract for children to comprehend "while they are still dealing with personal hygiene" (Hicks 1991).

Others worry that children understand environmental problems all too well. They see children as unfairly burdened by concerns about global warming and nuclear disaster and believe children are emotionally and psychologically overwhelmed by environmental problems far beyond their measure of social influence or control. Research on children's responses to the threat of nuclear war refers to "nuclear nightmares" and the "psychic numbing" of children (Mesnikoff 1989). Cynicism, apathy, and even nihilism among children has been reported as the direct result of "nuclear overload" (La Farge 1987). Phyllis La Farge reports that many children are "restricting their emotions," retreating into private or religious-fundamentalist worlds and withdrawing from the political process (74–75). They are depicted as "survival artists" trying to cope with intense vulnerability and "learned helplessness" in the face of nuclear proliferation (89).

But others portray "environmentalized" children in a quite different light: as overzealous, intolerant, and self-righteous "eco-enforcers" "harassing" their parents to stop eating meat, turn off the water, stop smoking cigarettes, and recycle the trash. Some express concern that children are responding to environmental messages by becoming rigidly intolerant of any human weakness (Coles 1986:243–79; Quindlen 1990). In the popular press, images of children as ecotyrants are promoted with headlines such as, "Parenting in the Nineties: The Winds of Ecological, Dietary, and Social Change Have Transformed Parenting. Haven't They?" (Shahin 1994) and "Kids Are Becoming Proselytizers for the Environment" (Boccella 1991).

Still other adults are troubled by the emphasis environmental-crisis messages place on changing patterns of consumption. They ask whether concern for the well-being of the planet will motivate children to participate as fully actualized, self-managing citizens in cooperative, ecological democracies[1] or whether children are simply learning to be "caring" consumers in a vast, global, "green" marketplace (Bookchin 1990; Coward 1990).

Children Drawing Their Concerns about the Planet

In view of these conflicting notions about children's environmental concerns, I decided to use children's drawings as a means of casting a wide net to discover what variety and kinds of concerns children might have about environmental crisis. Drawings, I have found, provide a relatively quick and easy way to gather social information from and about children. Teachers and camp directors are generally cooperative, and on the whole, children are not only willing but are eager to participate in drawing sessions.

While conducting my study throughout the summer and fall of 1991, I gathered drawings from 325 children between the ages of five and fifteen from three elementary schools, three summer camps, and one neighborhood center in upstate New York and from four elementary schools in South Carolina. Most of the children were white, working class or middle class, and under twelve years old. Black children within the same age and class range were also represented, as was a subsample of low-income black children from a small blue-collar city in upstate New York. Also included were children attending special-education classes (these account for most of the children over eleven years old), two Chinese-speaking children, two wheelchair-using children, and a child with Down syndrome.

I asked children to draw a picture about what it means *to you* when someone says, "You have to help save the planet." I held no discussions before drawing sessions, except to introduce the activity as part of a project on children and saving the planet. Sessions lasted approximately twenty to thirty minutes, after which I gave the children an opportunity to discuss their drawings in a group setting, asking them, Can you tell us what is going on in your picture? I tape-recorded or copied these brief (approximately five-minute) discussions onto the back of each child's drawing and used them later for content analysis. Because some children drew more than one picture, I collected a total of 354 drawings. I used all of the drawings to construct thematic categories, but only a child's *first* drawing to compare across grades, gender, race, class, and geographical region.

Using a qualitative method of content analysis, I analyzed each picture, in an attempt to discover categories of children's environmental concern (see Glaser and Strauss 1967; King 1994), sorting drawings according to subject choice, and whether or not they contained human figures, signs of environmental damage or problems, and positive or negative environmental slogans. Gradually, I saw piles of drawings take on distinctive characteristics—a particular emotional and/or environmental theme. Patterns emerged, leading me to construct six categories of children's environmental concern: Everything's Okay (10 percent), Taking Personal Action (47 percent), Calling for Action (21 percent), Depicting the Problem (9 percent), Indicting the Problem Makers (10 percent), and Recasting the Problem (<3 percent).

Overwhelmingly, these drawings indicate that children are very much aware of environmental crisis (87 percent). And, remarkably, nearly half of all the children (47 percent)—including 67 percent of the kindergarteners and first-graders, and almost half of all the girls (47 percent) and boys (47 percent)—depict themselves or others taking personal action for positive social/environmental change (see Tables 1 and 2). Drawings and follow-up interviews show that while some of the children express a daunting awareness that it takes power and effort to "save the planet," many children feel empowered rather than unduly burdened, by the call for global stewardship. Detailed descriptions of each category follow, illustrating different aspects of children's environmental awareness and concern

TABLE 1   THEMES IN CHILDREN'S DRAWINGS BY GRADE

	Grade			
	K–1 (%)	*2–3* (%)	*4–5* (%)	*6–8* (%)
Everything's Okay	8.5	21.8	3.6	0.0
Taking Personal Action	63.9	37.3	55.1	28.1
Calling for Action	10.6	18.2	27.7	46.9
Depicting the Problem	2.1	10.9	8.0	15.6
Indicting the Problem Makers	12.8	7.3	10.9	9.4
Recasting Problem	2.1	4.5	0.7	0.0
	100.0	100.0	100.0	100.0
	(n=47)	(n=110)	(n=138)	(n=32)

Everything's Okay. *The environment as a Garden of Eden, drawn by an eight-year-old girl.*

Everything's Okay   *A cheerful portrait of the planet by a nine-year-old girl.*

Everything's Okay   *A lovely landscape with a view of the earth, drawn by a seven-year-old girl.*

Taking Personal Action *Many kindergartners draw themselves saving the planet. This picture of children getting garbage out of the water was drawn by a five-year-old girl.*

Taking Personal Action *Using technology to save the earth. These girls in spacesuits were drawn by a nine-year-old girl.*

Taking Personal Action *A ten-year-old boy describes his drawing: "This little man is me going to tell the president to make an announcement about pollution. He should say that people who pollute the world should go to jail."*

Calling for Action *This before and after drawing of the earth, by a seven-year-old girl, is typical of many children's poster art.*

Calling for Action *An eleven-year-old girl uses peace signs and recycling symbols to make her picture of saving the planet.*

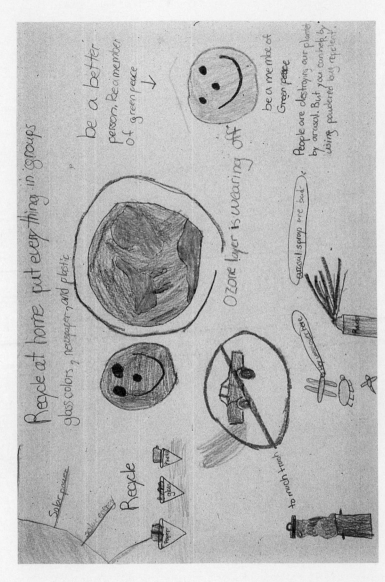

Calling for action *This ten-year-old boy incorporates a wide range of calls for environmental action in his drawing.*

Depicting the Problem   *A thirteen-year-old boy draws the earth as ugly and eaten away by pollution.*

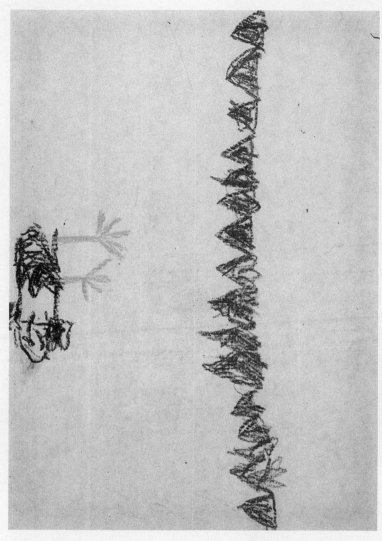

Depicting the problem *A bird flying with a plastic six-pack ring around its neck, drawn by a five-year-old boy.*

Depicting the Problem   *Many children depict litter on lawns as an environmental problem, as in this drawing by an eight-year-old girl.*

The factories are
polluting the air and water.
They should recycle
That would help

Indicting the Problem Makers *Like this six-year-old boy, many children draw pollution from factories as an environmental problem.*

Indicting the Problem Makers *For many children individual responsibility is the dominant theme of their drawing, as in this portrayal of a girl wasting water, by an eleven-year-old girl.*

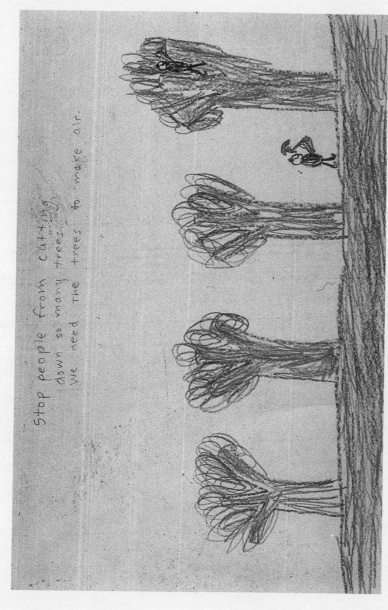

Stop people from cutting down so many trees. We need the trees to make air.

Indicting the Problem Makers *Like many children, this six-year-old boy depicts loggers as environmental villains.*

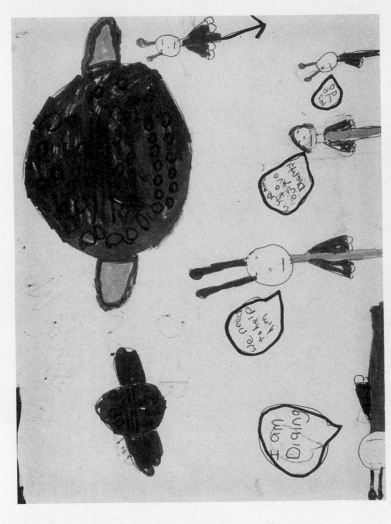

Recasting the Problem *A nine-year-old boy draws a dying alien from outer space, with an onlooker saying "We have to save our plantet [sic]."*

TABLE 2   THEMES IN CHILDREN'S DRAWINGS BY GENDER

	Gender	
	Girls (%)	Boys (%)
Everything's Okay	9.6	11.0
Taking Personal Action	47.1	46.7
Calling for Action	25.7	16.3
Depicting the Problem	11.2	6.0
Indicting the Problem Makers	4.8	17.0
Recasting Problem	1.6	3.0
	100.0	100.0
	(n=187)	(n=135)

and raising issues and questions of political and theoretical significance about their environmentalization.

Categories of Children's Environmental Concern

Everything's Okay

These drawings are imbued with an aura of deep tranquility. Each picture reveals an apparent absence of stress and evokes a quiet sense of repose. Reminiscent of the Garden of Eden, one young girl's picture is replete with butterflies, a deer, two smiling girls, and a fancy bird. Even an intricately drawn green-and-red-eyed snake is shown amicably curled around a sturdy tree. Nature is presented as serene, home as secure. Flowers, rainbows, trees, even a child's dark-cloud and rainy scene, conjure up the pastoral image of nature at peace and in balance. People are curiously absent from these drawings, while animals, including among others a horse, dog, birds, turtles, snakes, and frogs, are more frequently represented. When they appear, homes are happy-looking places, nestled in a landscape devoid of any indication of problems, pollution, damaged ozone layer, or recyclable trash.

Almost half of all these drawings include some rendition of a healthy, happy planet earth. In one engaging variant a nine-year-old girl draws the earth as a smiling global figure wearing top hat and flowers, with a continent for a nose, and arms and legs that protrude from its benign rotundness. Many children portray the earth in space amid other planets in the solar system, while others place it high or low in the horizon, often right between simultaneous depictions of the sun and the moon.

Assuming that these children are unaware of environmental crisis, we might expect a correlation between that lack of awareness and chronological age and grade, with the youngest children representing the least environmentally aware. This is not borne out in the present study, however. In fact, more second- and third-graders drew unpolluted nature scenes than did the youngest participants, kindergarteners and first-graders (see Table 1).

Given the undeniable ubiquity of environmental-crisis messages to children, it is significant that those in the (relatively) higher grades are overrepresented in a category that seems to imply total innocence or blissful obliviousness about "saving the planet." Perhaps the appellation "Everything's Okay" is too simplistic to adequately describe this kind of environmental concern. Could it be these children are *too* aware of environmental crisis and are expressing psychological avoidance, fanciful escape from overwhelming, stressful "planetary" demands? Perhaps. But there are reasons to doubt such a conclusion. The content of these pictures evinces much pleasure in natural scenes. And there are virtually no indicators of the bizarre or the strange—content that might reasonably be expected in representations of children's repressed fear. Another reading—going beyond the apparent, yet consistent with the content of the drawings—suggests that these idyllic scenes might depict the world put right again, after the work of saving the planet has been done.

Perhaps these children are painting a portrait of a world worth saving, a motivational goal for would-be "Planeteers." This is supported by the comments of one third-grade boy, describing his pastoral scene: "It's a forest with a waterfall and a river really clean, and it's nice and clean and there's no garbage on the ground." Another child, whose first drawing depicts smiling figures picking up garbage (and therefore is not included in the Everything's Okay category), drew a second picture of a house, a bird, and a flower. About her first picture she reports, "This is the earth, and this is Pluto. And here is me; I'm cleaning up all the garbage and putting it into the wastebasket. And there's one more piece [of garbage to pick up]." Referring to her second picture, she says, "This is it all cleaned up. And I'm inside, playing with my friends."

Although such examples suggest that some of these children *are* responding to environmental concern, if at a subtle level, it is still possible that many are simply unaware of environmental crisis, for when asked about their drawings, most failed to directly mention any specific environmental problem or issue. Thus, despite some ambiguity between the content and descriptions of their drawings, children in this category appear to be unaware of any crisis in "save-the-planet" messages.

Taking Personal Action

Almost half of all the children in this study drew pictures of themselves and/or others actively participating in some kind of environmental activity; if not, the artist provided clear, spontaneous verbal comments indicating that such activity is implied in their picture. One child's picture of a landscape, with objects circled and slashed with a line, illustrates this latter type. The eight-year-old girl describes, "There's a whole bunch of junk on the ground and I pick it up. . . . I made a ["no"] sign." Several of the younger children express their personal action in their comments, though not in their pictures.

Almost two-thirds of the kindergarten and first-grade youngsters drew and/or described themselves in environmental activity (see Table 1). Examples include releasing dolphins from underwater cages, stopping people from capturing animals in the rainforest, "help[ing] elephants live forever so they don't do what the dinosaurs did (they all died)," and picking up garbage, including on the moon: "I went to the moon when I was two

years old. They have garbage there too. I helped pick it up."
These youngest children (five- and six-year-olds) exhibit a remarkable, if idiosyncratic, awareness of environmental issues,
along with a marked sense of personal agency in the face of
global problems.

Teaching or enlisting others to help save the planet is a common theme throughout the drawings in this category. Describing his picture—a bright and smiling figure bending cheerfully
to pick up an object—one five-year-old boy states, "I went outside and found some poison that bad boys left on the ground. It
was sickness poison. I put it in the garbage. Kids should learn
from their parents that poison is bad." This is a rare example of a
child directly citing parents as socializing agents. More typically
these children depict themselves as socializers "environmentalizing" others, as for example, in a fifth-grade South Carolina
girl's drawing of two smiling girls and a scowling male figure, of
whom she wrote, "The girls are showing the man to not pulite
[*sic*]. Throw trash in the trashcan." Throwing away trash and
picking up garbage are dominant themes here, with 60 percent
of the drawings including some rendition of people personally
"cleaning up" the environment.

All the children whose drawings make up this category depict
themselves and/or others performing some kind of constructive
action to improve environmental conditions. There are, however, qualitative differences in the ways they render the degree
of effort required to "save" the planet. Although many draw
smiling, cheerful figures busily picking up garbage or recycling
trash, a few children (7 percent) add representational details or
dialogue that underscores the hard work they perceive to be
necessary for getting the monumental job done. Preparing to
clean up a messy park, one little girl in a drawing tells her
friends, "We better put our shoes on." "Whew!" a girl in another
drawing declares. "All of this work I did will pay off." "It means
it's a difficult...," a boy writes at the top of his page. "Yuck,"
protests another child's figure, working at sorting and picking
up trash. Several children draw figures wiping sweat from their
brow, and one picture in particular seems to sum up the theme
that saving the planet is hard work. Smiling bravely, a little girl
holds the entire earth on her back. "The fate of the world is on
our shoulders," the fifth-grader's heading declares.

A perfectly equal gender division occurs in this category, with almost half of both the girls and boys drawing someone taking personal action to help the environment (see Table 2). Some gender differences in theme preference can be detected, however, with more girls drawing "protecting, preventing, and nurturing" themes—such as planting trees or saving animals—while only boys depict "avenging" as a way of taking personal action. The two instances of avenging polluters include a figure with a gun "kill[ing] Captain Dirt Man" and a huge hand holding a pistol, shooting "the Litter Man." Recall Ellen Seiter's (1993) discussion of gender difference in children's cartoons of "saving the world from toxicity" in which she points out that cartoons aimed at boys employ the traditional plot of "direct battle with a villain using a weapon," while cartoons aimed at girls promote "teamwork" (1993:159). In light of the very different themes aimed at girls and boys, it is interesting to note how few boys actually drew pictures of themselves or others using weapons to fend off toxic villains, whereas both girls and boys frequently depict themselves and others working together as a team to clean up the earth.

Girls and boys also draw themselves using technology to repair environmental problems. Technical solutions range from the pleasantly mundane (vacuum cleaners suctioning up garbage from the surface of the earth, children sweeping the planet with brooms) to the celestial. In one third-grader's drawing, two girls in spacesuits, attached by thick tubes to their rocketship, approach the planet crying, "I will help the Earth!" In another, the power of the sun is used to propel a young boy's solar car. One child, a six-year-old boy, uses a brightly striped hot-air balloon to depict himself picking up beer bottles floating in the sky against the backdrop of a multi-ringed planet.

Throughout every thematic variation, which includes one instance of a child (a black boy from South Carolina) walking up the steps of the White House to inform the president about "bad polluters who should go to jail," the dominant response to environmental concern is a sense of personal agency. These children unambiguously convey, in visual and/or verbal terms, that they feel they *can* do something about the "problems with the planet." The meanings and implications of this kind of environmental empowerment for children remain to be examined.

Calling for Action

One is immediately struck by the persistent use of the imperative in these drawings, as over and over the viewer is exhorted
to "HELP SAVE THE PLANET!" and "MAKE OUR EARTH A HAP-
PIER PLACE!" Words take on special significance in this (the
second-largest) category of children's environmental concern,
in which drawings are distinguished by an absence of human
figures and a surfeit of positive slogans and signs demanding
environmental action. The dominant message is a rallying cry to
others to eradicate environmental problems.

For some children pure symbolic gesture is used to persuade
others to participate in environmental activism. Many children
simply draw recycling cans, or even more succinctly, the circular arrows of the "reduce, reuse, recycle" symbol. Several incor-
porate the circular symbol of the peace sign along with the
recycle sign or with a picture of the earth. Most children combine images of environmentalism—planets, recycling cans, and
natural landscapes are the most common—with words, slogans,
and text. In some pictures the text threatens to overwhelm, as
in one twelve-year-old girl's drawing, which contains almost half
a page of written commentary:

> Q: What do you think of when someone says you have to
> help save the planet[?].
> A: Recycle. Pick up trash. Try to help people be aware of
> problems such as the holy [*sic*] ozone. If you see a piece
> of litter pick it up.

Other children "plant" signs in their pictures' front yards,
reminiscent of local election campaigns, with pointed messages
about the environment. The slogans below are from individual
signs in a drawing by an eight-year-old girl:

> "Recicle!" [*sic*]. "Help save our earth!" "You can save our
> animal friends by saving their homes." "Don't ploute
> [*sic*]." "Save rainforests." "You can help us save the
> earth." "Have composts!"

Drawing posters or signs rather than human figures in action can be interpreted as a kind of political activism: "Another aspect of children's art [recalls] the traditional function of poster art and the traditional prerogative of such serious and renowned and diverse artists as Goya, Kollwitz, Picasso, Hopper, Remington . . . [to convey] social comment [and] rhetorical assertion" (Coles 1992:49). There are several ways children take this political stance in their drawings about environmental crisis. Some try to educate their viewers, using their drawings as a way to show others proper environmental actions. A fourth-grade South Carolina boy demonstrates a remarkable knowledge of environmental issues in his drawing, including suggestions for positive actions such as using solar energy and joining Greenpeace.

Other children use "before-and-after" techniques, dividing the page into two frames, with the earth (or a landscape scene) depicted first as polluted or damaged, and then as repaired or cleaned up. "See what happens when you don't take care of the Earth," one fourth-grade girl writes. Then, "See what you can do when you clean up." This can also work in reverse, as in another fourth-grade girl's drawing, "Make your world a better place [smiling, green-blue planet] . . . not worse" [orange-and-brown planet "all steamed-up" emitting red rays and an angry grimace].

Many of these children demonstrate political commitment and concern in their pictures of "saving the planet." But another, more complex, quality emerges when drawings in this category are taken as a whole. Revealed in the repetitiveness of content and tone—the incessant imperative, the sameness of the slogans, the planets, the message—a sense arises that for some politics is reduced to a treacly slogan on a Hallmark card: "Saving my planet means a lot to me. Tell me what saving your planet means to you [fill in the blank]." Perched atop a pretty rainbow and a shining sun, this second-grader's sentiment can easily be reduced to "cute."

Similarly, the sheer redundancy of virtually interchangeable depictions of the earth with "Recycle," "Save the Earth," or "Save the Planet" at the head suggest the possibility of contradictions here—commitment and trivialization, impassioned pleas and pat phrases, social comment and social reproduction—in the expression of some children's environmental concern. Paired and contrasted with "taking personal action" drawings, they raise complex questions about issues of children's empowerment and political engagement, and the social uses of environmentalization.

Depicting the Problem

A distinct qualitative shift occurs in the content and mood of these children's drawings. Looking at them, one is left with a tangible sense of warning, anxiety, and foreboding. Here environmental problems are depicted without any sign of personal action, perpetrators, or solutions. "If we do nothing the planet could look like this!" one seventh-grade boy declares beneath a ragged-edged, orange, black, and purple earth. "No polluting or the animals will die," a third-grader warns. Pictures of planets with bites taken out or with garish colors are a recurrent image, as are garbage-strewn rivers and fields. Several children, girls and boys alike, depict bombs exploding, some as pulsating abstract energy, others as mushroom clouds complete with "BOOM!" and "BOSH!" sound effects and children crying "AH!" or "SUE! SUE!" (The artist, an eight-year-old girl, explains that "Sue" is a person, not a legal action.) One kindergartner, an Asian American boy from Brooklyn, describes the bird in his drawing as wearing "one of those soda rings around his neck." The happy-looking home from the Everything's Okay category is mutated here into an anthropomorphic figure wearing Band-Aids and a fiery roof crying "HELP!—SAVE OUR HOME," a frowning face in the "O" of the word "our."

Confronted with personal responsibility to save the planet, these children respond with graphic images of decay and destruction, things gone wrong, the ecosystem awry. Significantly, none locate any agent of decay, no specific causal factor in the problems they depict. Nor do they find refuge in Arcadia, satisfaction in slogans, or power in personal action. Of course, it is important to remember that each category represents only one kind of response children may have to environmental-crisis messages. Individual children may draw second or third pictures from completely different perspectives, reaffirming the commonplace that we all are capable of holding simultaneously contradictory notions (and emotions). Still, the drawings here clearly reveal that at least some children, at some times, respond to messages about global environmental crisis with serious worry, without easy or immediate recourse or relief, and without any apparent awareness or understanding of the root causes of the problems with which they are being faced.

Given the somewhat "negative" cast of these drawings (emphasizing problems without indicating solutions, or providing only warning slogans), it is interesting to note the grade, regional, race and class, and gender differences that appear in this category of environmental concern. Drawings from the youngest children (kindergarten and first grade) are virtually absent (the kindergartner's drawing described above—of a bird with a plastic six-pack ring around its neck—represents that child's second drawing), whereas those of twice as many sixth- to eighth-graders as might be expected by chance are represented (see Table 1). Similarly, regional differences arise, with four times as many northern children (12 percent) as southern children (3 percent) drawing environmental problems without solutions. Race alone does not appear to be a significant factor in these children's depiction of environmental problems, but when race is combined with class, twice as many poor black children (five of seventeen—29 percent) draw problems than would be expected by chance. There also appears to be a trend in gender differences, with more girls and fewer boys emphasizing environmental problems (see Table 2).

Why do more girls and poor black children draw problems without solutions than do boys or white children? These findings are suggestive, pointing to a relationship between social marginality and perceptions of empowerment. For those children whose drawings suggest a sense of personal power, virtually no differences correspond to gender or race and class. However, for those children who express a sense of *powerlessness* in their drawings of saving the planet, differences in race, class, and gender come into play. These children's drawings indicate that while membership in a socially marginal category (girls, poor blacks) does not necessarily create or cause a felt sense of powerlessness in children, it may increase the *likelihood* that children will feel (or at least, draw themselves as) powerless to do anything about "saving the planet." If we take into account the inverse—the more powerful gender in a society thinks powerfully; the more powerful race and class in a society thinks powerfully—intuitively this makes sense.

Generalizations from these drawings need to be carefully qualified, given the small numbers and the study's nonrandom sample. Even so, they raise theoretical implications of an intersection of race, class, and gender issues in the environmentalization of children, implications that merit further consideration.

Indicting the Problem Makers

Again, drawings here focus on environmental problems—not solutions, personal actions, or calls for change. However, these drawings are distinguished by pointing out the problem makers and indicting those considered responsible for creating environmental problems.

Air polluters rank as the most frequently represented environmental culprits, symbolized by billowing smokestacks of nameless factories; car, truck, and jet plane exhaust; people burning garbage or trash; and even radioactive emissions from a nuclear-power plant. Some children point to users of aerosol cans as direct destroyers of the earth's protective ozone layer. (None drew the store where the aerosol cans are sold, or the chemical plant where the offending ingredients are developed and produced.) Other commonly cited problem makers include people who cut down, destroy, or otherwise damage trees; water polluters; and garbage dumpers and litterers.

One picture features a frightened- (and frightening-) looking character at a computer terminal. The artist, a fourteen-year-old boy from a special-education class, explains: "It's a scientist working on a computer. We need to send messages to all the scientists in the world telling this, 'Don't mess up the environment or we won't have one.' Scientists ought to think of more ways to save the planet than rockets and bombs." This child's drawing is a mixture of indictment and recruitment. Scientists are cited as creators of "rockets and bombs" and other (implied) technology that "mess[es] up the environment." At the same time, scientists are depicted as having an express responsibility to "think of ways to save the planet."

Few children specifically cite personal representatives of corporate capitalism or nation-states as responsible for environmental damage, although one girl draws the *Exxon Valdez* spilling oil into the sea. More common are nameless oil tankers and anonymous smoky factories emitting air pollution and dumping toxic waste. In yet another (dramatic) depiction, a whaling ship is shown trying to capture and kill a great whale.

For many children individual responsibility for environmental crisis is the dominant theme of their drawings. "A lot of people think only about themselves. They need to think about the Earth," states one kindergarten boy, drawing two menacing figures carrying chainsaws toward a tall tree. "If you don't recycle water you will not have any. . . . Turn the water off," an eleven-year-old girl admonishes, the child in her picture brushing her teeth while leaving the water running, oblivious to its rapid depletion.

These children see artifacts, not owners, of capital and technology—factories, vehicles, aerosol sprays, workers, and consumers—as primarily responsible for environmental pollution. For example, loggers or others who cut down trees are a frequently cited culprit, perhaps in response to messages about saving the rainforest and old-growth forests in the Northwest, and the much publicized controversy over the endangered northern spotted owl. But few children directly name institutional polluters, although the Alaskan oil spill by the *Exxon Valdez* has left its trace in many of these children's drawings. It appears that contrary to those in the Taking Personal Action category, whose drawings in general depict ecoproblems as individually created and resolved by "you and me," children in the Indicting the Problem Maker category display a budding awareness of the institutional origins of environmental crisis but offer few, if any, structural solutions in their drawings.

Although grade level seems to be significant in children's preference for depicting environmental problems (older children are much more likely to emphasize problems than are kindergarten and first-graders), they do not appear to be a factor in children's depiction of problem makers (see Table 1). However, a developing pattern of race, class, and gender differences in children's drawings of environmental-crisis themes continues here, with almost three times as many boys as girls drawing pictures depicting environmental problem makers (see Table 2), and no poor black children drawing problem makers. Keeping in mind that this category of concern represents a small percentage of drawings by children in the study (10 percent), it still appears that race, class, and gender play a role in children's understanding of environmental-crisis themes, particularly for those children who do not draw themselves or others taking some kind of personal action to "save the planet."

Recasting the Problem

These drawings represent a very small number (less than 3 percent) that seem to dramatically change or recast the intended "save-the-planet" message. Unlike the first category (Everything's Okay), in whose drawings the planet itself is the element that seems to leave the clearest trace (and thus fuels speculation that the message has been understood on some level by children drawing those pictures), here it is the "saving" part, or the depiction of some other kind of danger, that is most evident.

These drawings are intriguing in the diverse ways they appropriate the notion of danger and saving the earth. One unique, somewhat inscrutable, drawing, by an upper-middle-class, fifth-grade black girl from coastal South Carolina, fills a page with the gaping mouth of a huge Jawslike killer whale, brilliantly colored in green and blue, with an impressively rendered double set of razor-sharp white teeth. Two other drawings, both by younger girls from different summer camps, depict a figure drowning. In one picture a child sits in a small wooden boat with a long ladder falling into the water. Another smaller child is apparently struggling in deep water near a black life preserver floating on the surface of the lake. "Save the eerth [*sic*]" the smiling girl in the boat cries out.

Aliens or creatures from outer space are a common theme, particularly among boys. One third-grader, a nine-year-old black boy from South Carolina, drew a picture that features two ringed planets in the sky, with several alien creatures involved in a set piece. "I am diaing [*sic*]," calls a prostrate, antennaed alien. "We need to help him," another alien impassively replies. A woman dressed in orange calls out, "We have to save our plantet [*sic*]." "Yes we do," the small extraterrestrial next to her responds.

Several of the boys' drawings depict planetary dangers and rescues in aggressive and militaristic terms. Two third-grade boys drew pictures of ships under attack by airborne enemies descending by parachute or magic cape. In another, the earth is shown under assault by extraterrestrials who are fiercely resisted by flying creatures with blazing rockets, "Tring [*sic*] to save the earth." Unlike the drawings in the category Taking Personal Action, these pictures—though action-packed—lose track of the notion of environmental crisis.

These "defenders-of-the-earth" drawings might be completely missing the intended message environmentally minded adults are seeking to convey. On the other hand, they may be demonstrating an implicit continuum of cultural messages that children, and especially boys, are getting from commercial cartoons and environmentalist rhetoric. In the context of "saving the planet" some children are primed to see not only the environment but the entire universe at stake. As Tom Engelhardt notes, cartoons such as *He-Man* and *Masters of the Universe* engage young children with the thrill (and chill) of Star Wars military technology, along with ads for innumerable action-figure toys that are equally, if not more, aggressive (1987:89–94). As I discussed in Chapter Two, the "enviro-tainment" cartoon *Captain Planet and the Planeteers* cleverly exploits this lucrative market for action figurines, blending the universe of the action-figure Superhero and plots about preventing environmental destruction with a vast merchandising and licensing enterprise.

That so few children recast "saving-the-planet" messages suggests that the environmentalization of children is an extremely effective project. The next chapter explores children's *experience* of environmental crisis and what it means to kids to be "green."

4

■

What
It Means
to Kids
to Be
Green

It's like grownups are so worried about money, so worried about, um, paying the mortgage, and keeping the
bills up to date, that they don't, they don't even, I don't
know, they don't seem like they have enough time. But
what happens? This is what I tell my parents all the time:
What happens when the planet blows up? You're not
going to have to worry about stuff like that.
                          —A twelve-year-old working-class girl

I have shown, children are very much aware of environmental
crisis. This comes as no surprise when we look at the proliferation of messages children are receiving about saving the planet
and at the many media representations of children as ecological activists and environmental police. But not only are
children aware of environmental crisis, they feel personally
responsible to do something about it. Their drawings indicate
that they are cheerfully willing to do their share to save the
planet. But what does saving the planet mean to children?
What feelings, attitudes, beliefs, and values constitute the sense
of empowerment that so many children express in their drawings of saving the planet? What do children understand environmental problems to be? Whom do they see as most responsible

for causing environmental crisis? And what exactly do kids think they can *do* to help save the planet?

"Picking Up the Earth"

Individually and in small groups, at summer camps, schools, parks, and neighborhood centers, I asked children what it means to them when someone says *they* have to save the planet. Across a range of ages from prekindergarten through preadolescence children's responses were remarkably similar: saving the planet means picking up trash. Five-year-old curly-haired Rubin told me, "It means that you can't leave garbage all over the place." Six-year-old Robert with the bright blue eyes said, "Clean. I would clean the garbage off my lawn." Sean, seven and just finished with first grade responded, "Yeah, I um did it a lot. Sometimes I'm picking up garbage when nobody even sees me. And um ... I do walk around and stuff picking up the earth." "Picking up the earth," including *other* people's garbage, is a recurrent theme for children. As nine-year-old Shane reports, this is a task children willingly take on:

> SHANE: Sometimes I pick up garbage at my grandma's house, or my grandma's [where] she babysits, they always, if they have like a cookie box they throw it on the ground and I have to go picking it up.
> DONNA: So you have to go around and pick up other people's garbage, that they throw on the ground?
> SHANE: I mean I want to.

Eleven-year-old Billy, from a middle-class black family, connects housekeeping and "earth keeping":

> Well that means that ... you should keep the planet clean so the planet don't get dirty or like waste stuff or anything. We should keep our planet clean, like we clean our, like [we] keep our house clean. It's like the same outside from our house. We should keep our stuff clean,

and our whole planet, so the planet won't be dirty and full of garbage and everything.

Dressed in faded cutoff blue jeans and a baggy white T-shirt, thirteen-year-old Shannon reaffirms the theme: "Well, it's like the earth is our home, and if it gets trashed, you know, we have nowhere to go. . . . So it's up to us to take care of it."

The Meaning of Garbage

Over and over the theme recurred: children feel personally responsible to keep the earth clean. But what is the meaning of garbage for kids? Jane, a six-year-old white girl, one of three siblings who along with their mother are surviving on welfare in a suburban neighborhood, sees cleaning the earth as directly related to a looming problem of overcrowded landfills: "Well I think everybody should help each other clean up the planet a little, because all this garbage is getting the planet all filled up and by the time everybody throws their garbage out it's going to be fulled [*sic*] up with garbage and there'll be nothing to really do for it." Claudia, nine years old and from an intact upper-middle-class family, associates garbage with disasters: "I have a book that, um, it's called *Great Disasters,* and it [says] that most of the great disasters that have happened include lots of garbage and stuff." The theme of household garbage as hazardous and even potentially deadly is vividly portrayed by nine-year-old Shane, the child who "wants to" pick up trash:

SHANE: So like an animal, like a duck or something, when there's like a soda can wrapper [plastic six-pack ring] and it comes around and it gets its neck caught in it, it grows bigger and bigger and then it chokes him and pretty soon he won't be able to eat or breathe and he'll die.

DONNA: Shane, where did you hear about stuff like that, the soda can wrappers?

SHANE: When my classroom, I went on a trip and I went to this place and it told us all about how garbage can do dangerous things to like animals or fish.

While most children associate garbage on the ground with dire consequences for the planet and its inhabitants, at least some children see litter as more a matter of personal tidiness. Middle-class mores that require suburban lawns to be tidy and clean are neatly incorporated into an "environmentalist" theme. Michael, a seven-year-old black Hispanic boy from an intact, lower-middle-class family, reports that his mom, dad, brother, "usually almost everyone," tell him to save the planet.

MICHAEL: Because we usually get the house dirty, they want us to clean up and sometimes there's litter outside, so we pick it up.
DONNA: Oh, so if your mom or dad see litter on the ground, they say that you have to help save the planet by picking up that litter?
MICHAEL: Um hm. Or usually they don't have to say it, we just do it.

Jennifer, an eleven-year-old who recently moved with her mother into her soon-to-be stepfather's upper-middle-class neighborhood, directly links saving the planet with the upkeep of private property.

DONNA: Tell me what that means to you, that you have to help save the planet.
JENNIFER: Um, by taking care of your garbage and respecting other people's property, and not throwing garbage on it, and respect how much you're putting in the garbage. And if you're just putting in like maybe like just stuff that could be recycled then that would be like not helping the planet at all.

The theme of recycling garbage is a common refrain in children's responses to saving the planet, and one children often tell each other. In the interchange below, eight-year-old Sandy urges her friend Meg, who already knows about picking up trash, to recycle.

MEG: Lots of people throw like tires and garbage and beer cans, stuff like that. I think we, people, should pick them up and throw them away.
SANDY: They shouldn't throw them away, they should recycle!
MEG: They even threw a dog away. Yeah, it was [wandering along] the side of the road, and we kept him.

Often children conflate the generic term "garbage" with a wide variety of environmental problems. Ten-year-old Megan, freckled and sporting a bouncy ponytail, incorporates environmental themes of cleaning, recycling, a dying planet, and danger to animals in her description of the hazards of garbage:

MEGAN: [Saving the planet] means recycling because, um, our planet is dying from all the smoke and gas from the garbage on it, and that's bringing us [trouble]. And some of the plants and animals are dying from the garbage.
DONNA: Where have you heard about saving the planet?
MEGAN: From my mom.... We always clean up the yard because people just throw things in our yard and think that the animals won't get it. Because we have a garden and the raccoons and chipmunks.... We have a chipmunk, and he eats everything. And I'm afraid the chipmunk's going to eat the garbage and then one day we'll find him dead.

Garbage is sometimes depicted as a direct cause of holes in the ozone. Nine-year-old Clarence and ten-year-old George are both working-class white boys going into fourth grade.

CLARENCE: Like you have to pick up garbage. You have to make sure you don't like throw your stuff on the ground because there already is a big giant hole in the um ... um ... what's it called again? [Several minutes later] The ozone layer! That's the one, that's the one. That's the word that I was thinking of.

DONNA: So the ozone layer has a hole in it.

CLARENCE: Yeah, a giant hole ... and we have to fix that up by not throwing garbage and stuff.

GEORGE: Not by that, not just by that. The hole is the size of the earth, they [say] it was bigger than the earth.

DONNA: Wow. But what can kids do about something like that, George?

GEORGE: Stop dropping the garbage all year long.

Conversely, ozone can be depicted as protecting the earth from garbage and other pollution. Eight-year-old Martha lives with her mother, father, and baby sister in a working-class neighborhood.

DONNA: What is the environment?

MARTHA: The environment is the earth, and you have to help the earth. Oh, and it's the ozone layer.

DONNA: And what is the ozone layer?

MARTHA: [shrugs her shoulders in a gesture of uncertainty] I think the ozone layer's like the top of the air where we are right now and then the rest is empty of the ozone layer. I think it's supposed to protect where we are right now from polluting and trash and stuff.

DONNA: Where did you hear about the ozone layer?

MARTHA: Mostly on TV. . . . The news channels mostly. . . . Sometimes I want to see what there is, what I should wear, but they go into ozone layer and stuff, and I watch that until they say what the weather's going to be like.

"If We Don't Watch Our Step . . ."

While picking up litter and recycling trash are dominant themes in children's perception of environmental crisis, as we can see, they are by no means the only problems of which children are keenly aware. Just a few of the environmental concerns cited by children include depletion of natural resources ("don't waste water, it's a lot big waste"), ozone depletion ("the ozone layer, it's just like dissolving"), medical-waste pollution ("needles and glass in the water"), air pollution ("dirty air" "smoky skies"), deforestation ("chopping down trees"), species extinction ("the loss of animals"), oil spills ("that big oil spill that took place in Alaska"), disappearing rainforests ("the rainforest that's burning"), toxic-waste pollution ("like the toxic wastes being dumped into the ocean"), military pollution ("like in the war, Saddam Hussein put all the oil in the ocean"), soil contamination ("paint on the ground soaking into the dirt"), global warming ("the greenhouse effect is just going to get hotter and hotter"), desertification ("they cut down all the plants and trees and the ground is dying"), nuclear contamination ("people who live downwind from the test site keep getting this radioactive fallout"), and water pollution ("dead fish floating up because of the oil spill").

A few children mentioned "too many people" as an environmental problem. Dillon, a thoughtful and serious eight-year-old with cropped blond hair and a freckled face, is entering the third grade. His mother recently remarried, and he has three siblings at home. Although he lives in a working-class neighborhood, both of his parents are medical doctors.

> DONNA: Is there anything else I didn't ask you about saving the planet that you'd...
> DILLON: [breaking in] Um, how many people, um, children you have.... Because there's too many kid[s], people on the planet. The earth takes up more stuff and more trees would have to be cut and stuff like that would happen. And more houses would have to be built... and the oceans would expand...
> DONNA: Hmm, so where do you think you've heard about there being too many people?
> DILLON: Discovery Channel. A lot of, in China there's a lot of, lot of, lot of people.
> DONNA: Hmm, they [the Discovery Channel show] talked about that?
> DILLON: They [meaning the Chinese] tried. Their goal is to have one. One child.

DONNA: Do you think when you grow up you're going to want to have children in your family?
DILLON: Um, I might. I . . . don't know.

Implied in any discussion of population control is the issue of abortion. While seemingly difficult for children to comprehend, this theme is introduced in a group interview by lithe and lively nine-year-old Allison, whose third-grade class celebrated Earth Day the day before. Having in mind the ecological notion of "the web of life," I asked the small group of children, "Are people part of the environment?" Allison immediately responded:

ALLISON: People are part of the environment . . . and we have to watch our step when we have, because like if we have so many people on this earth, we're not all gonna fit on it. That's the main idea about this earth. If we don't watch our step, we're not gonna be able to fit on this earth.
DONNA: What can people do to watch our step?
ALLISON: Well, I mean, you can, I don't mean like bornishing [*sic*] people or things like that . . .
DONNA: Like *what* people?
ALLISON: Um . . .
MARLA: Abortion.
DONNA: Oh, abortion?
ALLISON: Yeah. [giggles from a few in group]
DONNA: You don't mean like getting rid of people before they are born, or anything like that.
ALLISON: No, 'cause that's an indivisional [*sic*] person . . . and . . . [pauses]
DONNA: So how are people gonna watch their step?
ALLISON: Well, maybe, I don't really know but, I mean . . . [pauses]
DONNA: So you know that there's a problem, maybe too many people, but you don't know exactly what people can do about it.
ALLISON: Do about it, yeah, because it's um, I mean you can't destroy them because that's, that's, I don't know, I just . . .

TIMMY: [The earth] will be too full, or like there's going
to be cities and no countries, cities all over the world,
apartments, everything.

DONNA: Do you think there is enough room on this
planet for everybody?

TIMMY: I, yeah . . .

ALLISON: Nope.

TIMMY: No, no, not if we . . . For now, for now it's okay,
but as soon as they get, as we multiply . . . the earth
doesn't get bigger.

DONNA: Where have you heard about too many people
on the earth?

ALLISON: Well we heard it from our class when we
talked about Earth Day yesterday, that there's, there's a
lot of people . . .

MARLA: I've heard some problems on the news . . . like in
the lakes, and they're polluting, and they're like using
motorboats.

Malthusian constructions of death and life meld into problems
of recreational vehicles discharging gas and oil into summer
vacation lakes. The abrupt juxtaposition of diverse and complex
environmental issues mirrors the "channel-surfing" mode of television viewing as a modern medium of information. Specifically
addressing electronic media in advanced-capitalist society, Douglas Kellner (1987) argues that television images are "fractured"
and "saturated with contradictions" that open spaces for diverse
readings. But while children are getting the message that there
are "too many people" in the world, they are not apt to hear how
inherently *racist* are Malthusian constructions of overpopulation. Similarly, when children learn that a fetus is an "individual
person," they are rarely, if ever, given a political and feminist
context in which to understand the abortion debate.

Sometimes there is spillover of other social-crisis themes in
children's concerns about saving the planet. Both eleven-year-
old Latitia, who is black and lives in a poor neighborhood under
foster care, and Charles, who is the same age, white, and from a
working-class family, link environmental problems and illicit
drug use.

LATITIA: You help the planet to be a better place [by] like stop polluting and try to prevent people from polluting. And you have to try to stop people from doing drugs and killing people.

DONNA: Charles, what do you see as some of the worst problems with the environment?
CHARLES: Littering, smoking and stuff, and drugs.

Preadolescent children I talked to who are poor, working class, and/or black are more likely to combine environmental problems with other social concerns. Examples such as these among children's drawings also suggest there may be a relationship between the variables of age, race, and class, and concerns about homicide, smoking cigarettes, alcohol, and drug use within a broadened theme of saving the planet.

"It Makes Me Feel Sad; It Makes Me Feel Mad!"

Children are aware of environmental crisis, and they want to do something about the problem. But how do children *feel* when they are told to save the planet? Writing in an early handbook of research methods in child development, Leon Yarrow notes: "There is a tendency for children in middle childhood to exclude adults actively from their private world. Unlike preschoolers who often think out loud, in the middle childhood period children are more likely to keep their feelings and thoughts to themselves. . . . Language is used very little at this age as a means of expressing feeling. It tends to be used almost exclusively in the service of the communication of ideas" (1960:566).

One of my earliest questions about children's experience of environmental crisis had to do with their emotional responses. Initially—because *I* felt that way—I thought children might feel overwhelmed or burdened by calls to save the planet. I thought that saving the planet might be perceived as too great a task, environmental crisis too massive a problem for children to confront without some kind of emotional distress. However, when I studied children's drawings of environmental crisis, I was surprised to discover that many, if not most, children express power to do something about saving the planet. Only 29 of 325 children (9 percent) drew pictures of environmental problems without any obvious solution or perpetrator. It seems, as Rosalind Coward (1990) tentatively suggests, that environmental messages about saving the planet have affected children in a "positive" way, fostering both a sense of personal responsibility and personal empowerment. However, I want to look carefully at the question of children's emotional responses to saving the planet. Is Yarrow correct in his assessment of "middle" children (eight-, nine-, and ten-year-olds) as "naturally" unwilling or unable to talk about their feelings? If he is wrong, and children can and do express their emotions, in this case about environmental crisis, what are they feeling?

Some children are reticent or perhaps simply uninspired to express their feelings about having to save the planet. Nine-year-old Justin informed me that at school his teacher had talked about holes in the ozone layer. But when I asked him how that made him feel, he whined and replied, "I don't know." Six-year-old Tara was taciturn in response to my emotional probing:

DONNA: How does it make you feel when someone says you have to help save the planet?
TARA: Pretty good.
DONNA: Pretty good?
TARA: Yeah.
DONNA: Anything special about it?
TARA: Um. Nah.

When children used monosyllabic phrases to answer questions about their feelings, I did not press on. I tried not to fill in for them by asking questions like, Does it make you feel happy or sad? assuming that to ask direct questions about particular emotional states would lead them too much in their responses. This reticence on *my* part might have limited my access to children's "environmental" emotions. Fortunately, however, most children I talked to, both in small groups and in individual interviews, were relatively forthcoming about their feelings. Across a range of ages children expressed a variety of emotions about having to save the planet.

For some children saving the planet makes them feel good, productive, and up to the task. Eleven-year-old Jennifer, seated on an embankment and fishing in a murky pond, explains:

> I mean, I think Camp Summer is a beautiful, beautiful camp because they, we always take care of the planet. Because we have like five minutes where everyone picks up garbage, everyday, the whole camp, we pick up garbage, each people. And um, I think that's really good. We pick up straw wrappers . . . and . . . at the end of the day [the camp director will] say, What is the cleanest area? and that sort of like makes you wanna do it, because you get the cleanest award. . . . They don't give an award, but they say the person who had the cleanest area was [so and so] and that feels really good because you know that what you are doing, people see. So that's good.

I've introduced Jennifer before—she lives in an environmentally active family with a soon-to-be stepfather who is a member of Greenpeace. Jennifer doesn't think *Captain Planet* is "down to earth" enough because the cartoon implies that only "superpeople" can save the planet, and she disagrees, asserting that "regular" people do the work of cleaning and recycling, "respecting private property," and not throwing trash on other people's lawns. Clearly, Jennifer feels good about doing her share to save the planet. However, some of the children I talked to were rather mixed about what is expected of them in their environmental roles. When I asked eight-year-old Evan, with his mass of dark-brown hair and his dark-brown eyes, how he felt about saving the planet, he expressed ambivalence and frustration at messages about recycling the trash.

> DONNA: Evan, how does it make you feel when you see all this stuff on TV about [saving] the planet?
> EVAN: Well, um, pretty good but sometimes, like, um, sometimes it's good and sometimes it's bad. Because somethings should be recycled but they say they're not going to be recycled. . . . And then the next time you see

them they might say they are going to be recycled. And then they keep saying this, and you're going to get mixed up, and like not remember one thing and then another.

How many adults have struggled similarly, trying to follow variable, and seemingly arbitrary, requirements in their communities for separating trash? Some places—upscale neighborhoods in the northeastern United States, for example—go so far as to employ "garbage police," whose sole function is to search residential curbside trash bags for illicit "recyclables." JoAnn Gutin (1992) exposes ironies inherent in current recycling myths and measures. Gutin argues that despite an elaborate coding system and much industry-generated publicity and hype, plastic remains essentially unrecylable. "Amassing a pile of plastics big enough to be worth something costs more than making it in the first place. It's almost impossible to escape the conclusion that recycling plastic is difficult and nearly pointless" (1992:58).

The inconsistencies, if not downright deceptions, of environmental public-relations campaigns are not lost on some children. Eight-year-old Claudia and nine-year-old Sally, listening intently to Evan's analysis of televised recycling injunctions, respond:

> CLAUDIA: But on TV, they don't always tell the truth on TV. They might just say something and they don't really mean that they're going to do it. I mean TV, it's not like they tell you the truth all the time.
> SALLY: Yeah, lots of commercials, they just lie to get you to buy their project, product.
> DONNA: So even when you hear stuff about the environment on TV . . .
> CLAUDIA: [cutting in] It's not always true.

When I asked children what it *means* to them when somebody tells them to save the planet, I often heard about environmental problems such as too much garbage on the ground and how children are responsible to clean it up. But when I asked children how it makes them *feel* to have to save the planet, contradictions inherent in notions of environmental crisis as "everyone's fault" were exposed: many children expressed frustration and anger at the legacy of pollution and environmental destruction left them by adults. Lee and Sara are thirteen-year-olds from middle-class families, Randi is twelve and working class. I talked to them one bright, sunny afternoon at a Girl Scout summer camp. Lee, with her dark-rimmed glasses and halting speech, appeared shy and circumspect. However, she expressed complex feelings about having to save the planet, moving beyond simple wariness of environmental hype to a full-scale condemnation of corporate producers.

> SARA: You feel like, if *you* don't do all this recycling stuff, you feel guilty.
> RANDI: Why are *we* paying for it?
> LEE: Yeah I know, it's just, sometimes you think, why should we? You know, as the kids we get all the hype and all this stuff about the recycling and . . . But why should we be doing most of it? Because we didn't have anything to do with it. I'm sure that most of the kids, if we ever had a chance to go back, we wouldn't create . . . all the plastic and stuff that they like throw away. But I think like grownups should do, especially like, you know, the people who like own the factories and stuff, they should do more.

Pretty, blond Randi, youngest of the three girls, was fiery and passionately outspoken about environmentalism. She expressed pointed anger toward "big businessmen," whom she sees as responsible for causing environmental damage.

> It makes me really mad when people say, or when you hear these big businessmen [say,] "Everyone out there should try to help save the environment." They reach in and do . . . recycling laws, they say all this stuff, and those guys are the ones going home drinkin' outta styrofoam cups [and] throwing 'em, you know, not recycling. It makes me mad when people realize that, they finally just woke up, they just realized that we're killing the ozone layer, we're killing all sorts of plant life. They're going

and dumping oil in the Persian Gulf, I mean you've gotta be a little looney to do that already. But you're killing everything, and people just woke up and realized it.

While Lee is clear about whom she sees as the environmental culprits ("*We* [kids] didn't have anything to do with it. . . . Grown-ups . . . especially . . . the people who like own the factories and stuff, *they* should do more"), Randi's shifting pronouns imply complicated feelings of guilt and blame that are at once directed toward others and experienced as personal ("*They* just realized that *we're* killing the ozone layer. . . . *You're* killing everything, and *people* just woke up).

While some children feel unadulterated anger or anger mixed with vague feelings of guilt, other children experience anger mixed with sorrow, loss, or fear at the prospect of inheriting a rapidly diminishing planet. Michelle, Jamie, Amy, and Julie are all eleven years old:

MICHELLE: It makes me feel bad, sad. Sad that people are so stupid to do this to our planet.

JAMIE: It's sad that the planet's being wasted.

DONNA: What do you think it will be like when you grow up? Do you ever think about that?

JAMIE: No.

MICHELLE: Sometimes I think if people keep on doing this, it will be like we won't even have a planet.

AMY: [It will] be like with gas masks to breathe when you grow up and like lots of trash.

MICHELLE: And really smoggy and . . .

JULIE: Sometimes it's getting so crowded everywhere, everybody'll have to live like the Jetsons.

Jamie, who feels sad that the planet is being "wasted," finds it difficult, perhaps impossible, to contemplate the consequences of environmental crisis for her future, while her friends envision a smoggy, poisonous, and overcrowded world. Third-grader Howie, slightly overweight and described by his teacher as a "loner," envisions pollution as not only hurting the earth but potentially shortening his own lifespan:

DONNA: What does it mean to save the earth, to you?
HOWIE: Well if you don't save the earth, you won't have an earth.
DONNA: So how does that make you feel, to think about that?
HOWIE: I don't ... it doesn't make me feel very good. Because I'm just nine years old and pretty soon [when] I ... hit forty-two, if this keeps up I won't be here for forty-three.
DONNA: What are you thinking it's going to be like when you're forty-two?
HOWIE: It's probably going to be very smoggy and stuff like that.

Some children describe feelings of panic when they hear about environmental crisis: Darren, Megan, and Mina are ten-year-olds in a fifth-grade special-education class.

DARREN: It makes you feel bad that the earth, all the fish and the dolphins and that, are dying.
MEGAN: Sometimes it scares me once and a while when you hear it in school—the planet and the ozone layer and everything's burning up and the rainforest. It really gets your heart beating fast because you don't know what's going to be happening to the earth.
MINA: Because if we have no earth, we can't move.

Nine-year-old Allison, concerned that "we'd better watch our step" with overpopulation, is frightened by the negative consequences of environmental pollution.

To me it means that um I want to live in a clean environment. I want the sky not to be smoggy, and I want the land to be clean, and I don't want oil spills in the ocean. It gives me a scary feel; if we don't clean this earth up we're gonna live in a junky place. And it's not gonna, it's just, it feels really scared to me, 'cause I don't want to live in a junky place. I want to live in a clean and beautiful environment.

Often in expressing concern about the planet children refer to the uncertain fate of future generations. Twelve-year-old Noah, in a sixth-grade special-education class, explained:

> It makes me feel scared. I'm thinking like maybe when my children grow up, and my children's children, maybe they'll go through the earth and they'll see orange all over, you know, the sky's all black or something, and maybe like the ground's all brown, you know. It makes me wonder. You try to, like whenever something's wrong, pick it up. You know, basic things like that.

Thomas, thirteen, and in a seventh-grade special-education class, expressed bitter cynicism in the face of future environmental destruction:

> THOMAS: If we don't [do something about the environmental crisis] it could look like my picture. Pitiful. Ugly.
> TEACHER: How does it make you feel?
> THOMAS: In a way I don't really care because it won't be by the time my life time is over.
> TEACHER: What about your children?
> THOMAS: They'll have to deal with it. You take it one day at a time. Probably by then they'll be living in space stations or something. Then when everybody leaves, the earth's gonna clean itself up over billions of years. Then they'll [be] coming back.

Randi is certain that future generations of children are innocent of environmental wrongdoing but will suffer for it just the same:

> This is going to sound conceited but I really am concerned. 'Cause I don't want my great-grandchildren to have to worry about this. I want, I don't think that they should have had to because they're millions, that's too far, but they're a few generations ahead and *they didn't do it.* The people back there did it, the people now are doing it. Not, not them that's going to come ahead. Maybe they'll add to it. But it costs, they say it costs too much money to do stuff like [repair environmental

problems]. Well then maybe they shouldn't have done
it in the first place.

As we have seen, the grammar children use when explaining
environmental responsibility indicates a sense of interchange-
ability, or perhaps better put, *interconnectedness:* "Maybe *they'll*
[future generations] add to it . . . but *they* ["big businessmen"] say
it costs too much money," "I think *we, people,* should pick up
trash," "How many *people,* um, *children* you have . . . there's too
many *kids, people* on the planet." However, the interconnectedness children feel is easily exploited in the service of a *diffusion
of responsibility* that tries to make environmental crisis everyone and no one's fault. Many children view environmental crisis
as somehow a direct result of their own neglect or wrongdoing.
George and Clarence, two working-class white boys cited above,
provide a perfect example of this paradoxical response to environmental problems:

> DONNA: How does it make you feel when you hear
> about the ozone layer?
> GEORGE: It make me feel, like, it makes me feel uh kind
> of mad and stuff.
> DONNA: Who do you think you're mad at?
> GEORGE: Me, really.
> CLARENCE: Like everybody.
> DONNA: [to George] What'd you say?
> GEORGE: Like me.
> CLARENCE: Like everybody.
> DONNA: [surprised] Like you?
> GEORGE: Yeah.
> DONNA: Mad at yourself?
> CLARENCE: Yeah, for making the big hole.
> GEORGE: Everybody, it's like mad at everybody, at like
> everybody . . .

Clarence, who has been trying to say that *everybody* is responsible, finally ends up confirming George's notion that *he* is
responsible for creating "the big hole" in the ozone layer.
George, in turn, becomes "mad at everybody." The comments of
these working-class boys epitomize a common liberal dilemma,

feeling a vague sense of personal guilt for massive, systemic problems whose cause and solution lie largely outside the boundary of any individual's immediate control. And they are not alone. Many children see themselves as responsible for the problems on the planet.

"It's Everybody's Fault; It's Nobody's Real Fault"

In Chapter Two I discussed contradictions inherent in liberal environmentalism, including the notion that we are all personally and equally responsible for generic "pollution." This is reflected in many children's interviews:

DONNA: Who do you think is most responsible for the problems on the planet?

MICHAEL [six-year-old black Hispanic boy, going into second grade]:   Um, people. That's all.

DONNA: People? And do you think there are some people who are more responsible than others?

MICHAEL: No.

ABE [eight-year-old white boy, going into third grade]: Well everybody, really. Like everybody is responsible for what they do. And if they like throw garbage on the ground, they're responsible for that.

KATIE [eleven-year-old white Hispanic girl, going into seventh grade]: There's holes in the ozone layer, and the trees are being planted and you know they're dying and everything.

DONNA: And who do you think's responsible for all that?

KATIE: I think the people are, because . . .

DONNA: Which people?

KATIE: I think everyone is . . . [because] we were not aware of it, we weren't aware of it before.

DONNA: Who do you think is responsible for most of the problems on the planet?

SHANNON [thirteen-year-old white girl, going into eighth grade]:   Everybody.

DONNA: Everybody equally, do you think?
SHANNON: Probably.

The paradoxical individualism of American culture is transparent here. The collective "we," easily invoked when fixing blame for environmental problems, diffuses any penetrating analysis of exactly who or what might be the root causes of ecological destruction. When adults respond in this way it often serves as a convenient form of obfuscation, especially when espoused by those with a vested interest in maintaining existing social relations. But what does it mean for children to shoulder the blame for ecological disaster? Environmental crisis is a complex problem for which some children may not necessarily feel blame, yet they experience the burden, as does eleven-year-old Billy, who linked "earth keeping" and housekeeping.

> DONNA: Who do you think is responsible for most of the problems with the environment?
> BILLY: [pause] Everybody.
> DONNA: Everybody?
> BILLY: I think everybody, because the people, whoever the person that made up the mess, is responsible for . . . to . . . they should pick it up. Because we, like the people that didn't make up the mess shouldn't pick it up, or we have to because we have to keep our planet clean.

Of course, when a problem is "nobody's *real* fault" it becomes rather tricky determining who exactly is responsible for repairs. Children know they are being called upon to fix the planet, and for some this is experienced as an unfair burden.

Sometimes I asked children whom they see as *most* responsible for problems on the planet, pressing a bit further than on other questions. My goal was to see how far children would continue to shoulder environmental blame and whether they saw adults as somehow differently implicated in this seemingly universal ("everybody on the earth") guilt. Eleven-year-old Timothy is a case in point.

> DONNA: Who do you see as most responsible for the problems on the planet?

TIMOTHY: People.

DONNA: Do you think all people are equally responsible?

TIMOTHY: No, people that don't care about the environment. Like people that throw away, um, I don't know really . . . um, well mostly, well some people. . . . I don't know.

DONNA: Who causes more problems, kids or adults?

TIMOTHY: [long pause] Adults, I guess. . . . Adults get to do a lot more stuff, and they drive the cars so they're causing the pollution because they're having the cars. And like, just . . .

DONNA: And where do they get the cars from?

TIMOTHY: Factories! Ah hah, they make a lot of pollution. They're made by grownups. . . . Because kids litter . . . [but] plastic factories [are worse].

DONNA: What would you tell a plastics-factory owner? Do you think they would listen to you?

TIMOTHY: No. . . . Because you're putting their business down.

While at some times children see environmental problems ambiguously, as everyone's (and thus no one's) fault, at other times, such as in the case of Randi, they can be quite clear about their own guiltlessness and the relative responsibility of (adult) others.

What I get a kick out of is they say um, they aim Earth Day at little kids. . . . It's like, when people like will say to you well you have to, you know, *you* have to like clean up all the trash and you have to recycle or else the world will be bad or something. But you know if people, if people back, you know, like ten, fifteen years ago had done what we're doing now, it wouldn't be like this. They're sort of making it like it's our fault if we don't, you know, do it now.

Seven-year-old Sean is sure that *he* is not to blame:

DONNA: Do you think everybody hurts the earth the same?

SEAN: No. Well, I don't know. But um, I never throw out stuff. And I never did.

DONNA: So do you think some people hurt it more than others?

SEAN: Well . . . I don't think too much people hurt the earth but I think a lot of people didn't know and a little bit of people did.

Like Sean, some children know that it is not "everybody" but rather a small minority of people—who may or may not listen to reason—who are responsible for environmental crisis. Talking about his "save-the-planet" drawing, nine-year-old Burt reports:

I drew a picture of a factory and a man was running up these stairs telling the other man to stop the factory . . . because there was too much smoke going into the atmosphere . . . [but] I don't think he listened.

Other children cite specific individuals as culpable for ecological problems on the planet. Eleven-year-old Mark recalled the 1989 *Exxon Valdez* oil spill as essentially the sole responsibility of its hapless captain, Joseph Hazelwood.

Do you remember when that big oil spill took place in Alaska? [My teacher] was really disappointed. . . . We said that the driver, whatever he did, since he spilled it, he should, well he didn't help in any way, so he should have been in prison, because he hurted the environment.

Most children are at best only vaguely aware of the complex roles multinational corporations, militaries, nation-states, and the World Bank play in wreaking environmental havoc. But at least some children recognize the corporate nature of pollution.

MINA: The sky pollution comes from big factories that . . . like my uncle works in a factory and he burns, um, I forget what he burns, but he burns something that goes off into the air.

DONNA: How do you know about that?

MINA: Because once he was watching me and I had to go to work with him. . . . I saw it and it didn't smell too good either.

TAD: Recycling factories still let off smoke and pollute the air. They have to go melt all the plastic to make a new thing and what it does is when they melt it the smoke is still going out in the air and still polluting.

Other children sense that a major part of the environmental problem has to do with reduction "at the source." Francesca and Melanie are eleven-year-old girls going into the sixth grade.

MELANIE: Well I watch TV and stuff and I see all the commercials for all the Worldwatch or whatever it is and it just makes me think that we don't need [most of] that stuff [being sold on TV]. All it's doing is ruining the world, and if we don't have a world to use it, then I mean, we really shouldn't . . .
FRANCESCA: It's really useless if you don't have a place to use it.

These children's observations are supported by Gutin in her conclusion about the silliness of current recycling programs for plastics: "It begins to look as though the least environmentally costly strategy, despite the appeal of plastics *RecyKling* as a concept, is source reduction. In other words, boring old absti-nence" (1992:59).

Children are aware of environmental crisis, and in large mea-sure they feel it is up to them to save the planet. For some kids there is anger, regret, even bitterness at having to deal with prob-lems for which they are in no way responsible. Others recognize the role "factories" and generally nameless corporations play in creating environmental hazards, waste, and useless products. But for most children environmental crisis is everybody's fault. Chil-dren are quick to lay blame for environmental problems on a highly generalized (and thus effectively neutralized) "we." Kids seem to be shouldering responsibility on a par with adults. But what exactly do children think they can *do* to save the planet?

The Meaning of Empowerment for Kids

Many, if not most, children feel empowered to do something about saving the planet. Litter and garbage are featured prominently in their drawings and interviews, and they frequently depict themselves or others picking up trash. Thus, it comes as no surprise that for many kids "cleaning up," at least in theory, is seen as a meaningful act. Eight-year-old Jake and eleven-year-old Michelle speak for many children in their responses:

> DONNA: Well what are kids supposed to do to help save the planet?
> JAKE: Clean up and don't be a litterbug.

> DONNA: So what do you think a kid can do?
> MICHELLE: Pick up garbage. Like last year here [at camp] we had a contest to see who could pick up the most garbage.

Picking up garbage, and inversely, not throwing down trash are, as we have seen, dominant themes in children's experience of saving the planet. But for some children, going beyond individual actions and exhorting *others* to change their environmental habits is a necessary, if somewhat risky, ecological act. Amy, Melissa, and Jamie are eleven-year-olds in summer camp.

> DONNA: So what are kids supposed to do about [water pollution]?
> AMY: Stop littering . . . and if you see something, if you see someone throwing it in, you should tell them they shouldn't.
> DONNA: Would you do that?
> MELISSA: Yeah.
> AMY: [gesture of uncertainty]
> JAMIE: It depends on how the person is. If it looks kinda big or if it looks like it's going to go after you, I wouldn't.
> DONNA: Are kids supposed to tell grownups . . .
> All three girls in unison: Yeah, yes, yeah.
> DONNA: Would you do that?
> JAMIE: I don't know, it depends, because if we were by

the water and this person... I don't, you know, I don't
want them to throw me in, especially if it was green.
DONNA: So you might be scared to tell a grownup?
JAMIE: Yeah.
DONNA: But Melissa, you would say something?
MELISSA: And then I would run.

Benjamin, a bright and enthusiastic environmentalist who just
completed third grade, hails from a family of social activists. He
is the child who sees Captain Planet as appealing in his superhero vulnerability to pollution and other environmental hazards. When I met Benjamin he was taking a break from a busy
morning at summer camp. It was late morning when we sat
together in the speckled shade on large tree roots pushing up
out of the side of an eroding hill. Benjamin eagerly ate what
looked to be a hastily put-together lunch: plain cream cheese on
the end piece of a loaf of white bread, a single carrot, and a small
jar of juice. After introductions and a few pleasantries about
camp, I asked him about saving the planet.

DONNA: Have you ever heard anybody say you have to
help save the planet?
BENJAMIN: Oh yeah, I heard it recently. Just as much as
they do, I say it to other people, actually.
DONNA: Who do you say it to?
BENJAMIN: I don't know. Basically [to] people who I see
that are being careless. Probably they don't listen to me,
they just say, "Oh, be quiet," or "Shut up," or whatever
they say. They just brush you off. I just say it like if
somebody litters, then I go, "Hey, can you pick that up?"
and then they just say, "Ah, be quiet," or just walk away
[and] pretend they don't notice me. I don't know, sometimes it's not even that. Sometimes I'm just saying that
you can help. That you *can.* And I try to.

Like fiery Randi, Benjamin is passionate about environmental
issues and is willing to risk rejection and hostility to try to
change people's environmental ways. Despite their environmental resolve, however, most children are keenly aware of
the potentially unpleasant consequences they face when telling

others, and in particular adults, to stop polluting and start saving the earth. This awareness is reflected in the frequent use of the word "encourage" in most children's accounts of approaching adults about saving the planet: "Well, we can encourage our parents to recycle; we can recycle ourselves," "Try to encourage them to recycle and just try to pick up garbage around their place," "We can encourage people and we can pick up trash and stuff," "Well they can encourage their parents to like ride bikes and things to stop using their cars. Or encourage them to go on a bus which does waste a little money but still it's better for the earth."

Will adults *listen* to kids admonishing them to save the planet? Some children report success in changing their parents' environmental ways, as in the cases of eleven-year-old Melanie and thirteen-year-old Leah:

DONNA: Have you had any effect on your parents?
MELANIE: I'm getting them to recycle. My mother refused to recycle at first because it was too hard. But I made a deal with her as long as I went down and brought the bottles back and forth, then we could do it.

DONNA: What do you think a kid can do about something like the ozone layer?
LEAH: They can, they can do stuff on their own like they can stop using poisonous gases and stuff like that, and tell their parents about it and people about it so they can stop doing it.
DONNA: Do you talk to your parents about any of this stuff at all?
LEAH: [very definitely] Yeah, now we recycle because we didn't before and now we recycle like aluminum and plastic and um that's um usually it, that's all.
DONNA: And is that because of your idea?
LEAH: Yeah, well I heard it in other places and I came home and I was just saying that we have to help save the planet because pretty soon when we get older the greenhouse effect is just gonna, it's gonna keep gettin' hotter and hotter and we're just, we're not gonna be able to live here very long.

DONNA: And how did [your parents] respond?

LEAH: They, they did what they could. We started recycling, like a year ago.

Despite some successes, few children see raising adults' environmental consciousness as an easy task. For twelve-year-old Noah, who worries what the world will be like for his great-grandchildren, and for his schoolmate, ten-year-old Laura, adults just don't get it.

DONNA: Do you think kids are teaching their parents anything about [environmental crisis]?

NOAH: Umm, they try but they're thick.

DONNA: The parents or the kids?

LAURA: The parents, like sometimes I talk to my mom about recycling and she just like blows it off and starts talking about something else.

Eight-year-old Rex feels powerless to even *communicate* with adults.

DONNA: Can kids change the way adults treat the environment?

REX: [pause] No. I know I can't. But I don't know about other people.

DONNA: Why not? What do you think gets in the way?

REX: My dad. He never, when he, he never lets me talk a lot. I have to kind of, I'll say, "Mom," and then Dad comes in and says, "Have you seen my keys?" and I never get to talk.

Some children imagine resorting to the institutional authority of the police as a last resort for controlling adult behavior, as in the case of Abe, who just completed the first grade.

DONNA: Do you think that parents and other adults will listen to kids?

ABE: Well, some won't but some will.

DONNA: Who do you think wouldn't listen?

ABE: Well, um like . . . someone who likes to be bad and things . . . and throw things around.

DONNA: What do you think kids can do about people like that?

ABE: Um, like tell them to stop or something. And if they don't stop like tell the police or something.

As we have seen, the sense of powerlessness some children feel in the world of adults extends beyond environmental issues. But as eleven-year-old Charles, who blames himself for the hole in the ozone, demonstrates, with a little encouragement even children who feel powerless can begin to imagine changing adults' environmental ways.

DONNA: What do you think a kid can do to help save the planet?

CHARLES: Nothing.

DONNA: Can kids make adults do things?

CHARLES: No, but adults can make kids do things.

DONNA: Do you think that sometimes kids can influence adults, make adults look at some things in a new way?

CHARLES: [hesitatingly] Yeah.

DONNA: Like how?

CHARLES: They see somebody like their parents doing something that they are not supposed to. Telling them that that's not what you're supposed to do. Like if they threw paper on the ground. Because when they [the parents] were going to school they didn't know about littering and stuff. . . . Now that there's more people than a lot of don't know than know, then they can tell them.

Working-class Charles introduces a key element for social and political change when he points out that a critical mass of people who care about the environment can lend support to individuals trying to save the planet. Even children who are much more optimistic than Charles about their potential effects on adults' behavior recognize the need for strength in numbers, as does thoughtful and serious eight-year-old Dillon, the child who said there are "too many kids, people on the planet:"

DONNA: Do you think that kids can change the way adults are doing things?

DILLON: Yes!

DONNA: Uh huh. What do you think kids can do?

DILLON: Because they can try to make their parents stop using the car, they can try to make them get a bike. And they should try to make them [move] their job to be closer to the house. If like, if it's far away . . . it would be hard to get there by bike. And by the time they'd get there . . . they might be fired. So they should be closer and they should use a bike.

DONNA: And do you think that adults will listen to kids?

DILLON: If all the kids join together to try to help, um, that's a way.

Expressing a desire to go beyond changing their own environmental habits, or that of their family or peers, some children call for changes in the wider social and political community. Most commonly children view letter writing to politicians as the means to make these changes. Eleven-year-old Latitia, who lives in foster care and associates environmental problems with other social problems such as "killing and drugs" said:

Well, I think that [kids] should send like letters to different states. And like they should write to the president. And the president, if he could help us with, um, getting the earth to be a better place.

Benjamin, the nine-year-old environmentalist whose family actively supports many movements for social justice, shows a remarkable insight into the power children have to use themselves as a rhetorical tool for political change.

DONNA: So what do you think a kid can do about these big adult problems?

BENJAMIN: Well, basically do the same thing adults do. Write letters. . . . [As a kid] you have a little bit more power and a little bit more strength because, you know, you can *say* in your letters—like the adults can say, "Well, I don't want my kid to . . ." or "Come on, stop" or whatever—but we [kids] can actually say *we're* going to have to live in it. We can say for ourselves, "We have to live in it and we don't want to." ... [Kids] have just a stronger way to act on it, saying, "Well, George Bush, you're not going to be alive; we will be. We're going to be in this smoggy, coughed-up environment, and we don't want it."

Benjamin cogently argues that, more than any other social category, children have a powerful moral and ethical position from which to demand environmental justice—the inalienable right to inherit at least a livable, if not a clean and beautiful, environment. This righteous sense of indignation spurs many children, such as ten-year-old Max, to continue writing to the president, even when their calls and letters go unanswered:

MAX: Like some kids will just write, keep on writing letters to the president, like giving it to him, and saying like, "So and so, I want, like, you know um, to help the environment and, you know, do this and that." And if you keep writing then maybe it will help it a little. So they're trying to help; some kids are trying to help a little more.
DONNA: How did you hear about kids that are doing stuff like writing to the president?
MAX: In our classroom we get this thing called uh [a kind of] news, and we get it about the environment, um, once a month in our classroom. And it tells about kids and everything and what they're doing to help the environment. And about animals and things.
DONNA: That's interesting. Is that something you would do, write a letter to the president?
MAX: Well, yeah, I did it a couple times before, and I asked them to write back and I never got an answer.

As I have shown in Chapter One, images of schoolchildren writing letters to politicians as a classroom activity is one that strikes fear and outrage into the hearts of politically conservative ideologues. Conservative opponents of liberal environmentalism recognize the potential political influence children wield, and the prospect of environmentally politicized children scares the daylights out of them. Education for participatory citizenship in a liberal democracy is reconfigured by political conservatives as a dangerously subversive act, akin to child abuse. But when children experience small victories in their political campaigns, to what degree do anti-environmentalists have just cause for concern?

> MAX: And [in another letter] I was telling our city mayor maybe to put more garbage cans around, so the kids that like to help clean up could pick up the garbage and throw it in the garbage can. So somebody could go along every day and pick up the garbage.... Well, they're putting [out] a couple more garbage cans; I did get written back from the mayor of [our city]. And he put a couple more in around Broadway, that's where a lot of the trash is, that's where we walk by. It's kind of like New York [City], you see cigarette things and garbage laying all on the grass part and right next to the sidewalk.... And so the [garbage] pickup doesn't come every day, it comes every two days, when they pick up the garbage.

Max is the child who described environmental crisis as everyone's fault and "nobody's real fault," who realized that "there's no Captain Planet going to clean up the earth and make it beautiful again; it's up to us.... You know, we're the bad guys and we have to turn into good guys, I guess." While he shoulders unfair burdens placed on him for environmental crisis, Max responds, in the liberal tradition, by trying to work within the system, writing letters to politicians and trying to get the big people in power to listen. Individual empowerment does seem to take on new meaning when children see the direct and effective results of their social and political environmental efforts. These effects can range from the sense of accomplishment and recognition children feel at being part of the cleanest group area in a summer camp, to the satisfaction that comes from having calls to the mayor for a neighborhood cleanup campaign realized.

Some children, however, recognize that it takes more than individual actions to change environmental (and ultimately social and political) practices. And for at least some children, such as twelve-year-old Noah, activist organizing is seen as a necessary means of "getting the message out to people."

DONNA: What do you think kids can do to help the planet?

NOAH: Like pick up stuff. They could maybe plant a tree. You know, maybe kids could even draw signs and hang them all over the place, telephone poles, getting the message out to people.

DONNA: And who do you think needs to hear the message?

NOAH: Mostly the grown ups. [Children in the group nod their heads in agreement]

NOAH: Yeah, because the grownups think they're smart, but man, it's really weird. In some ways I think that kids are much smarter when it comes to the environment. [Vigorous head nodding among the group]

NOAH: I mean some people, they'd rather have a leopard skin then have their children grow up with a real live leopard to look at. Really, a lot [of] stupidity that is.

Those children who are committed to political and environmental activism such as nine-year-old Benjamin, recognize that organizing is not easy and that it is an ongoing struggle.

BENJAMIN: I keep trying to start stuff, like, I tried to start something but then three people in the group quit, no, actually two people in the group quit, there was only five people originally, so we ended up with three people in the group. Not much rules because it would be environmental subjects, working with the war on poverty, stuff like that. You can't really do it with only three people, so that was trying to built up.... I try to organize a lot of things; they just end up in pishaposh, nothing.

DONNA: Is this something that you do through your school?

BENJAMIN: No, no, no, just with my friends, anybody. Most of them [are] from my school because most of my friends are in school, but still I mean I take, I take them from another school too, but they just, somehow it falls apart and we never get to do it.

DONNA: What's your first step for organizing?

BENJAMIN: My first step is to ... gather people that want to do it, and find them out, and bring them. And I have my first meeting which is kind of boring. I go over, "Hey, this is serious. It's not the fun stuff." And then that's why most people give up. Because they don't like it; they don't like the first meeting. But I mean everybody's got to have the first meeting talking. You can't start a group going out into the field ...

DONNA: How did you get people together for a meeting about the environment?

BENJAMIN: Yeah, well you see ... me and my mom and all that, we had one, it was called the environment ... I forget the name of it [pauses to think]. Oh heck, who cares about the name? And we used to go out and do all sorts of science projects and stuff about the environment.

DONNA: So you mom's into saving the planet too?

BENJAMIN: Oh yeah.... We come from a family of activists.... Yeah, peace activists, democracy activists, everything, communists.... We go to demonstrations, vigils. The latest vigil that we've been doing is because they keep setting off bomb tests in Nevada. That's been our latest issue, I think.

Children such as Benjamin don't jibe with the negative media constructions of ecovigilante children self-righteously and fanatically proselytizing about saving the planet to hapless, harassed, and environmentally stupid parents. Contrary to popular representations of parents and children at odds, or even more dramatically, as reversing traditional authoritarian roles when it comes to environmental issues, in Benjamin's case, mother and child are sympathetic and in sync in their political and social commitments and concerns.

Conservatives such as Jonathan Adler are inclined to view such environmental and political engagement as the exploitation of concerned children by "ideologically motivated" adults. In the meantime, simplistic slogans and crass commercialism in liberal environmentalism *do* exploit children but in a completely different way—by (cynically or naively) selling children a false bill of goods and selling them short in terms of effective ecological action. It is a sad irony that liberal environmentalism for the most part subverts and contains the politicization of children by promoting individual solutions to systemic and structural, social, economic, and political problems.

However, as Douglas Kellner argues, while all American popular culture is rooted in a capitalist structure of profit and exploitation (and, I would add, racist and sexist oppression), contradictions always arise that leave room for many meanings, including emancipatory ones. In talking to Benjamin, who identified himself as politically active and who talked articulately and at length about his environmental concern, I never sensed the simple parroting of catch phrases of "politically correct" adults.

> DONNA: What do you think will really make [adults and politicians] listen?
> BENJAMIN: You know, at this rate I don't know if anything will. You know, as if all we've done isn't enough? And this is just the beginning. And all these, if you feel like [we've accomplished our goal with] a debate we've run, or [the] "End the styrofoam" [campaign] or whatever happened in those places, well, listen to this, that's just the beginning. That's almost just McDonald's and Burger King. That's just a little portion, you know. They still have a lot more. And then they just don't listen to it. And we know how much it took just to do that much. It took *years*. So either it has to speed up, or it's getting a little hard for them to listen to anything.
> DONNA: And when you say "them," who ...
> BENJAMIN: We mean basically the government because basically the government has most of the power to change. Because they have, they make laws, they're in charge of making laws. I mean, you could just make for your state, you could make it for your community. But that's not going really help, as much. It's better to go for the top. But, still ... it's usually easier to get you community [involved].

Of course, most children are not trained at an early age, as Benjamin has been, to view the world as a political arena in which long and hard struggles for power, and for environmental and social justice, are continuously fought. Many, perhaps most, children in the United States, particularly among the affluent white middle-class, live in a world "sheltered" from genuine political knowledge and grassroots organizing. But even "sheltered" children can recognize the *potential* for political power and the need for collective organizing.

With his sandy bowl-cut hair, slightly high-pitched voice, generic overalls, and calm demeanor, eight-year-old Toby is truly an androgynous child. An only child living in a semirural community, Toby attends a private school founded in the Waldorf tradition. There are no "grades," and children advance in their reading skill very slowly, sometimes not even beginning to learn to read until they reach eight or nine years, in accordance with the growth of their second teeth. Parents are told to avoid dressing them in neon colors or in clothes that sport cartoon characters, and the school requires that children watch *no* television at home, not educational shows on public stations or children's videos. The school aspires to be a rarefied world carefully designed to "shelter" children from adult culture, commerce, and concerns. The curriculum places heavy emphasis on fairy tales, myths, and nature lore.

> In school we also learn about the elementals. They're like the little spirits that help the earth . . . and . . . there are all kinds of gnomes; there's earth gnomes, then there's root gnomes. For instance, if you were pulling up a turnip and it just wouldn't come out of the ground, perhaps you've forgotten to ask the root gnome if you can pull it up. Because a lot of times they're hanging onto the roots. And they don't let you pull it up without their permission. But all you have to do is ask, and they always say, "Yes, you can take my turnip, you just forgot to ask me." So a lot of times, whenever I take flowers, I always ask a tree, or a plant, "Can I take your flower for my table?"

The magical respect for nature that Toby embodies is vehemently derided by social ecologist Murray Bookchin (1990) as unpolitical and potentially reactionary.

> The most recent tendency in the environmental movement . . . is completely ghostly and vaporous. Bluntly

put: it consists of attempts to turn ecology into a religion by peopling the natural world with gods, goddesses, woodsprites, and self-styled "wiccan anarchists." . . . Political activity and social engagement in this theistic terrain tend to shrivel from activism into quietism and from social organization into privatistic encounter-groups. (1990:162–63)

But despite fairy tales and root gnomes, and contrary to Bookchin's fear of a privatized and supernaturalized ecology, Toby is *social* in his environmental outlook and recognizes the need for collective action and peer modeling.

DONNA: What about you? What do you think that *you're* supposed to do to help the environment?
TOBY: Personally, I think that as a child, some of my friends also do this, where our school is, part of the Waldorf School is based on nature. So, what we do is, a lot of children in my class, we're one of the classes most connected to nature. So, we try and get other children in the school to stop constantly thinking about Ninja Turtles and so on. And to start thinking about what they can do to save all the elements and the environment.
DONNA: Do the kids listen to you?
TOBY: Sometimes they do.
DONNA: How do you get them to be interested?
TOBY: You show them the use of nature, and how much stuff you can do without having it man-made. In fact, one of the teachers was totally into nature, and he took them on nature walks, all kinds of things. He taught them how to build shelters out of trees that had fallen, and so on.

When Toby cites technology, and modernity itself, as the biggest problem with the planet, he refers to the earth as a kind of social actor that needs consideration and to collective action as the only way to help the planet.

Personally, I think that people have naturally become too modern. And there are too many machines going on now. . . . Earlier, when people first started to settle America, they should have listened to the Indians' warning: "Keep this place clean. Don't pollute it. Always ask if you are going to take something from the environment." And now they're realizing they need to do that. And parties are getting together and cleaning up.

Similarly, when I asked Toby what he would do if he were put in charge of the whole planet, he responded:

The first thing that I would do would be to gather a group of people together to help the environment. And they would barely use cars.

Like most children I talked to, Toby at first universalized environmental blame. But it soon became apparent that he knows that environmental pollution entails much more than litter on the ground and that children are not the culprits of ecological disaster:

DONNA: Who do you think is causing the most problems with the environment?
TOBY: [thoughtful pause] I think most all people in the world.
DONNA: Do you think some people are hurting the environment more than others?
TOBY: [immediately] Yes.
DONNA: Who are they? What are they doing?
TOBY: Well, people that work in factories, if someone complains about pollution, and the town, they say, "Well, look, you've got to make this product or that product, if you want it, you've got to put up with it." But, a way that they could, for instance, if a tire-manufacturing factory, there would be a lot of smoke, and that's because of the rubber and stuff that has to be put together to make the tire. If I complained, and the person gave me a bad answer, I would say, "One thing you could do is to try and clean up after you've done this. Or put some kind of air filter above the chimney." Something like that.
DONNA: So you would give them some ideas of how they might do a cleaner job. . . . Do you think that kids

can change the way adults use the environment or mistreat the environment?

TOBY: [instantly] Yes, I do, yes.

DONNA: Do you think that adults will listen to kids?

TOBY: Actually, you know, this is an interesting question, because if one kid were to tell a ... if one kid were to go up, or two kids were to go up to a Democrat and say [shouting for emphasis], "If you were elected president, please try and help the environment," I doubt the Democrat would really listen. But I was [carefully chosen word here] glancing at a television when I was visiting my grandmother, and a whole big group of children got together, and they went onto the television with microphones and everything, and they were talking to the Democrats. And one kid said, "Do you follow me?" He was talking about, "I will help save my environment," and [he was telling the Democrat] to like answer all, to repeat what I say. And he was doing all kinds of things like, "I will help my environment, I will protect the earth." And two of the Democrats did it. So, if a big group of children gets together, it would work.

DONNA: I think you've got a good idea. It must have been exciting to see that on television.

TOBY: And to actually see a child standing up there at a podium and everything, with a microphone, and there were four Democrats sitting at a table, actually *listening* to the children.

DONNA: Wow, that's pretty exciting.

TOBY: Um hm.

One of children's most immediate communities, from which they learn and through which they speak, is that of their peers. For some children an epiphany can occur when they observe groups of kids speaking in public forums to political candidates about children's environmental concerns. Children feel empowered by the dawning recognition that they are members of a political constituency and as such have voices that may be heard. Not insignifiicantly, Toby's political epiphany came via television, that much maligned medium that Neil Postman (1985) and others argue is "amusing us to death." The fact that popular culture is "fractured and saturated with meaning" is evident here. While *Captain Planet* and "green advertising" shamelessly sell useless commodities to kids in the name of "saving the planet," on the same convex tube children can experience for the first time a heady sensation of political empowerment.

But as Sharon Stephens (1992), representative of the Norwegian Centre for Child Research at the Global Forum in Rio, carefully documents, children's political efforts for social and environmental change are typically thwarted or ignored by powerful adults in local, national, and global political arenas.

> Many of the young people at the [Rio] conference expressed frustration with the official convention negotiations and felt that, while their presence was desired as a sign of the importance conference organizers placed on the participation of children and youth, in fact their views were not really taken seriously. This was clear, some argued, from the lack of a lobbying "treaty" specifically focused on children, youth and the environment. (1992:47)

However fleeting their effect on the environmental behavior of political candidates, still something profound is going on for many children who are concerned about environmental crisis. But as eleven-year-old Katherine explains, kids don't want to do it alone: "Yeah, but we need our parents' help. We can't just go out and do all this stuff. We need our parents help." Benjamin, sitting on a tree root, munching his cream cheese sandwich, takes a slightly different perspective on the matter:

> You'd be surprised. You think, oh well, the adults go around and have their meetings, and have their plans, and have their [takes a breath] things, but kids have almost as much power. Because we can go out and like organize a TV show with a little help.... It's hard, but still, it's just as easy for kids as for adults. We just need a little help with TV, or anything really special like getting in with the town hall or something [like that].... But otherwise they're almost, the kids, we can go out and

fund-raise on our own. Just have us, drive us somewhere, and we'll do the rest.

Benjamin's conclusion, "Just... drive us somewhere, and
we'll do the rest," has a certain poignancy. Something important
is going on here beyond the shouldering of an environmental
burden created by adults. The potential for a genuine children's
politics of environmentalism exists in the call to save the planet.
While for many children it remains at the vague and relatively
unformed level of "picking up the earth," the message holds
within it a radical potential.

> Some argued that there are structural reasons... for the
> difficulties young people had in being heard in Rio. Lo-
> cated outside global structures of power and influence,
> children and young people could put at the center of
> their discussions and initiatives the "politically inexpedi-
> ent" issues that remained on the periphery of the official
> UNCED talks and convention-making. The social dimen-
> sions of environmental problems that young people em-
> phasize, and the vivid, concrete ways they frequently
> express themselves, are unsettling and "frame-breaking"
> within the context of conventional national and interna-
> tional politics. (Stephens 1992:49)

The unsettling and frame-breaking quality that children can
bring to the political arena ("the emperor has no clothes!") is
one that needs to be nurtured and *heeded* by adults. Children
recognize this. But while the potential exists for a radically new
awareness that recognizes and responds to children's environmental and social concerns, for the most part children are only
being *used* across the political spectrum. In global forums and
around kitchen tables, children express bitterness at the ecological legacy left for them to both literally and metaphorically
clean up. Still, many children, like Randi, empathize with adults,
and particularly with parents, who are slow-going in embracing
ecology as a way of life.

> Like my parents, I mean, they do stuff, you know. I've got
> them... I'm always screaming at them for not doing

things. I'm always doing that. And we haven't been recycling. We were recycling paper but like we haven't really
put together a recycling program in our house. And I'm
like, I saw recycling bins on sale, [and] I'm like, "We're
going out and buying those." I don't even ask them because they know . . . they care, it's just there's a lot of
other things on their mind. . . . It's like grownups are so
worried about money, so worried about, um, paying the
mortgage, and keeping the bills up to date, that they
don't, they don't even, I don't know, they don't seem like
they have enough time. But what happens? This is what I
tell my parents all the time: What happens when the
planet blows up? You're not going to have to worry
about stuff like that.

In a world they are constantly called upon to save, children
are poised to bridge false and oppressive dichotomies between
public and private, masculine and feminine, global and local, and
even adult and child. Despite the best intentions of loving caretakers, children are rarely sheltered from adult concerns. They
have exquisite antennae that sense family tensions stemming
from money troubles, marital problems, unsatisfying work conditions or unemployment, aging parents, chronic illness, social
isolation, and so forth. When coupled with a persistent call to
save the planet, an enormous burden is placed on their shoulders. While they may feel empowered, we owe it to kids to
provide them with effective tools for dealing with the real
world. This does not mean, however, as Murray Bookchin would
have it, that we must ban water sylphs and wood sprites in favor
of Aristotle and the Englightenment. There is a meaningful (and
unavoidable) place for the irrational in human life, not only for
children but for adults as well. As essayist and science fiction
writer Ursula Le Guin writes: "Those who refuse to listen to
dragons are probably doomed to spend their lives acting out the
nightmares of politicians. We like to think we live in daylight, but
half the world is always dark; and fantasy, like poetry, speaks the
language of the night" (1982:1). However, as I have also tried to
show, *Ferngully* fairies and magical rings, recycling rituals and
lessons on greenhouse gases or toxic waste do not teach children *enough* how to effectively address and *change* oppressive

social conditions that are the root causes of ecological crisis. In fact, they often function to obfuscate and perpetuate unjust social relations. Even product boycotts and school letter-writing campaigns, decried by Adler and others as "political advocacy," operate more to *contain* than to promote radical impulses generated in children by environmental crisis. The deep *concern* that Randi and Benjamin, Toby and Max, Jennifer and Dillon, Noah and Allison, and many, many other children feel, not only for their own future but for the future of the planet, is potent and real. But the question remains whether that potency will be "channeled" into middle-class tidiness, caring consumerism, nihilistic cynicism, apocalyptic hedonism, "wiccan anarchism," or disruptive "frame breaking" in the global arena of environmental politics.

Conclusion

Children are not social incompetents when it comes to under-standing and interpreting environmental messages. Even very young children know what it means to "save the planet" and are responding to environmental socialization in often thoughtful and creative ways. Similarly, and in some ways surprisingly, most children are not experiencing themselves as vulnerable victims, hopeless and helpless in the face of overwhelming global respon-sibility. They are neither cynical nor apathetic—although older children are more likely to draw environmental problems with-out solutions than are younger ones, supporting evidence that children's political attitudes become increasingly negative with age (Palonsky 1987). Contrary to popular myths portraying eco-activist children as environmentally correct bullies, children are not terrorizing others with stringent, self-righteous, or unreason-able demands, nor do they generally express themselves in rigid or tyrannical terms.

Most children are responding to social messages about envi-ronmental crisis with a clear and confident sense that they can do something about the problem, either through some kind of personal activity or by urging others to do their share to save the planet. However, what is the meaning of this empowerment for children who experience it? What does it signify for the society that promotes it? And, should adults rest assured know-ing that children are feeling empowered in this way?

In the late 1960s, similar questions were raised regarding the effectiveness of political socialization in the schools. Sociologist Robert Hess maintains that children in the United States were being presented with a "picture of unity, equality, and freedom that ... is distorted, over-simplified, and, to a degree, false"

(1968:529). Schools, he argues, created "an attitude of complacency" and a willingness in children to embrace "inaccurate representations" of the nation as "powerful, wise, and of good intent" (531). Hess points out that a young child, socialized to believe, for example, in the power of the vote, learns nothing of the "realities of political influence... [and, consequently] overestimates his [*sic*] own power until he attempts to have an effect upon politics or institutions in government" (531). Hess also asserts that teaching democratic political values in the form of slogans, rather than as concepts to be applied to social issues, leads to superficial acceptance of egalitarian principles— principles that often disappear when lived social and political contexts require tolerance for the expression of opposing, controversial, or nonconforming views. Summing up his critique, Hess states: "In short, much of the political socialization that takes place at elementary and high-school levels is lacking in candor, is superficial with respect to basic issues, is cognitively fragmented, and produces little grasp of the implications of principles and their application to new situations" (532).

More than quarter of a century later, much the same issues arise regarding the environmental socialization of children. Children are cheerfully targeted for environmental concern. They are told to pick up the trash, recycle plastic, conserve trees and water, and buy "green" products. In this lifestyle context, saving the planet becomes a comfortable arena for feeling socially and politically committed, much better suited to white middle-class concerns than, for example, "brotherhood," with its inevitable, uncomfortable, acknowledgment of longstanding racist (not to mention sexist) oppression; or "nuclear winter," with its attendant gloomy focus on the international proliferation of military weapons of mass destruction.

Saving-the-planet messages accommodate capitalist social relations in an effective, if paradoxical, fashion. Pictures of the earth are plastered on commodities as diverse as T-shirts and toilet paper. Children as young as three and four are cultivated as a major consumer market (McNeal 1992), with environmentalism sold to kids in any number of ways. The discourse of environmental disaster encompasses a broad range of social, political, economic, biological, and cultural concerns. But the rhetoric of liberal environmentalism, expressed in cultural productions such as *Captain Planet*, and in the pat phrases of many children's environmental drawings, promotes the notion that global environmental degradation—the end result of multinational corporate, military/industrial, and nation-state practices of consumption and production—is really "everybody's fault." The reduction of complex, global problems to simplistic, individualist solutions serves corporate interests much more effectively than it does children, who are willingly accepting responsibility for stewardship of a planet that is, in most ways, not under their control.

Borrowing from Pierre Bourdieu (1977), one could argue that liberal environmentalism is a form of "symbolic violence," in which the consent of children is sought to maintain the hegemony of global capitalism. However, inextricably intertwined in the liberal-environmental paradox is the message to children that they *can* do something. Children are not "cultural dopes" (Hall 1981), passively consuming ideas and rhetoric supplied them by their elders and the culture at large. Children actively interpret, appropriate, and often subvert or resist messages aimed at them by society—whether they be from school, home, their friends, television, or the mall. A sense of empowerment, that actions have effects and words the power to persuade, is one many children in this study easily embrace.

Hess's caveat—that children supplied with a superficial sense of empowerment are being set up for a fall—needs to be heeded, however, in general and in the specific context of liberal environmentalism in the late twentieth century. In our current culture of easy empowerment, not *all* children feel the power is theirs. Race, class, and gender differences negatively affect the quality of some children's environmental concern, particularly when children *do not* directly express a sense that they personally can help "save the planet." Even when adults profess to "give" children "power," the road to empowerment is fraught with land mines and potholes, forks and twists and turns; where the road might eventually lead, no one can confidently predict.

It is undeniably easier to deconstruct the liberal-environmental paradox than it is to offer concrete alternatives for environmental change, particularly when talking about political practice and empowering children. This is so particularly in a postmodern world whose very foundation (if one can posit such a thing) rests upon the assumption that all foundations are fluid; all meanings, mediated; all certainties, provisional; all efforts at empowerment, "dangerous." Michel Foucault, that Zelig of current academic discourse,[1] posits that truth is inseparable from power: "Each society has its regime of truth, its general politics of truth; that is, the types of discourse which it accepts and makes function as true" (1980:133). This insight has contributed to a difficult debate about the possibility of empowerment. As feminist pedagogue Jennifer Gore (1992) argues: "In attempts to empower others we need to acknowledge that our agency has limits, that we might 'get it wrong' in assuming we know what would be empowering for others, and that no matter what our aims or how we go about 'empowering,' our efforts will be partial and inconsistent" (1992:63). If all truth is provisional and prone to promote the welfare of some social groups at the expense of others, the question arises. Can anyone act from the confident assurance that they have an "other's" best interest at heart? In such a frame of reference even "oppositional" critiques of power are open to question: "No discourse is inherently liberating or oppressive. . . . The liberatory status of any discourse is a matter of historical inquiry, not theoretical pronouncement" (Sawicki, quoted in Gore 1992:61).

But radical action for social and environmental change, one that enlists children and cares about their welfare, *depends* on creating and fostering a political community that shares values, beliefs, and a politics of *truth,* of what is good and just and fair and supportive of *life.* Bridging the gap between postmodern analysis of power and the pressing material need for radical social and environmental change might seem an academic exercise to grassroots activists working in the trenches of local environmental battles. But regimes of truth operate effectively to promote some possibilities and to cut off others, thus making discourse a fundamental battleground for social change. Our very concepts of what constitutes childhood, nature, difference, community are limited in large measure by the parameters of the prevailing "truths" that any historically specific society promotes. It is therefore a radical *political* act to deconstruct regimes of truth that history proves have led to environmental destruction and the systematic oppression of women, children, "nonwhites," and other "others."

Liberal environmentalism fails, I argue, when it neglects to critique thoroughly and vigorously the ideological assumptions inherent in our current social relations. A radically new set of social relations between humans and nature, and between humans and humans, is essential to rectify the environmental crisis we face today. This will require a highly politicized and socialized environmentalism, one that looks well beyond dominant ideologies of capitalism, patriarchy, racism, and liberal individualism. Environmentally sustainable economic systems must replace the free-market capitalism and vestigial state-sponsored socialism responsible for global environmental degradation. At the same time, new concepts of nature and humanity must be embraced, concepts that radically reconfigure our social and ecological relations.

In the liberal-environmental paradox nature is ambivalently theorized as both mother and resource. But neither mothers nor natural resources have fared well under a patriarchal capitalism rooted in an epistemology of nature as "other," to be feared, dominated, and exploited. Some notions of nature as Gaia can be politically reactionary, as in neo-Malthusianist biocentrism, in which a transcendent Nature dominates culture/"man" (Bandy 1992). But other theories of nature hold a subversive potential, as in the various forms of ecofeminism, in which nature and humanity are understood as inextricably linked (see Diamond and Orenstein 1990). Ideologies of patriarchy and capitalism, racism and liberal individualism forget or deny the simple yet profoundly radical fact that we (humans *and* nature) are interdependent. Contrary to Hobbes's assertion, humans do *not* "spring like mushrooms"; rather, we "grow out of connectedness" (Rothman 1994).

Some feminists argue that emphasizing interconnectedness with reference to women's reproductive capacity is a dangerous enterprise serving to keep women trapped in traditional and oppressive roles of nurturers and caretakers. There is good reason to take caution here. But the (re)cognition of our interconnectedness has the potential to be not reactionary but profoundly social. When we acknowledge, embrace, and *embody* interconnectedness everything changes; the ways we relate to each other and the earth, the quality of our consciousness, our concerns, expectations, priorities, how we do things. This women-centered approach is not the "natural" result of some essential, biological, or instinctual property inherent in *women.* "Women-centered" discourse arises in the face of a regime of truth defined by masculinist priorities. As Carmen Luke writes:

> Relations for men historically are oppositional and confrontational (e.g., the struggle with nature), instrumental (object-centered production, alienation from and exchange of commodities) and dominating (nature, other, life). The preoccupation with death and destruction is an historically and philosophically inscribed male valuation of the order of things.... By contrast... women's reproductive consciousness and potential, [our] connectedness to the production of life ... locates [our] experience of self and others in an embodied relation to and in continuum with life, not death. (1992:42–43)

But at the same time that we are embodied and interconnected we are also socially *constructed,* fabricated, made, and embedded in a complex cybernetic web. Donna Haraway argues this point in a postmodern politics of feminism and environmentalism.

> If the world exists for us as "nature," this designates a kind of relationship, an achievement among many actors, not all of them human, not all of them organic, not all of them technological. In its scientific embodiments as well as in other forms, nature is made, but not entirely by humans; it is a co-construction among humans and non-humans. (1992:297).

It is also, she might have added, a co-construction among adults and *children.* Despite the fact that their images have been widely appropriated, their consent vigorously sought, and their consumption carefully cultivated, children themselves, ironically, have rarely been central to environmental discourse. Those of us who care about the fate of children (and of the planet) need to put children's needs, not simply their images, at the center of the environmental debate. Children need fresh air, safe food, clean water, and a nurturing environment in which to live, play, work, and prosper. Less obvious, but equally important, children deserve respect and a measure of control over the social conditions of their lives.

Feminists frequently point to women as most vulnerable to environmental degradation, leaving implicit the effects on children. Putting children at the center of a radical environmental discourse, however, does *not* mean pitting their needs against those of women. Valerie Walkerdine cautions that in the liberal push for children's empowerment (what she terms a "fantasy of liberation"), women, as teachers and mothers, bear the cost as "servant[s] to the omnipotent child, whose needs must be met at all times" (1992:21). Walkerdine argues that women "feel guilty because the future and 'freedom of our children, forever' is laid at [our] door. [We] are the guardians of an impossible dream, reason's dream of democratic harmony" (22). The seemingly positive task of teaching children to be self-managing citizens in a liberal democracy is deconstructed by Walkerdine as a "sham" and "an impossible fiction," where "passion is transformed into the safety of reason" and "progressivism makes powerlessness, the product of oppression, invisible" (20–21).

The world *is* a dangerous place, and children need to recognize, and exercise, their power. At the same time, when children occupy the center of our discourses (environmental and otherwise), caring for them becomes the responsibility of the entire community, not simply of mothers, teachers, domestic workers, or un-paid nurturers. A politics rooted in communal caring must expand life-affirming actions and ideologies from a private to a broadly social concern. It is important to recognize that adults cannot "empower" children in any simple, straightforward, uncontaminated sense. All efforts at empowerment are "dangerous," provisional, incomplete, inconclusive, and headed for who knows where in the long run. Nevertheless, we who care about children have an obligation to take this risk, to work to eliminate social and environmental conditions that history has proved to be oppressive and deadly. Only in this way will the root problems that jeopardize both children and the planet be identified and addressed. Children, as prototypical framebreakers, can begin to show the way.

Notes

Introduction

1 WMHT, "Save It! Operation Earth." This 1990 environmental-essay contest was sponsored by PBS member station WMHT in Schenectady, New York.

1 Images of Children in Environmental Crisis

1 Colletti writes:

> More recent studies seem to have definitively cleared the field of two old commonplaces. The first was that Rousseau claims the "state of nature" as a real condition which actually existed, whereas this supposed "state" basically represents for him . . . a "reference concept," a hypothesis, a degree zero, by which to measure the "divergence" of each individual phase of human civilization with respect to the original conditions. The second, much more serious position, is that in his works Rousseau is inviting society to choose the savage existence rather then society ("He wants to walk on four legs," Voltaire wrote sarcastically.) This error . . . has survived from the eighteenth century to our own day, despite the warning in the *Discourse* itself, where Rousseau exclaims: "What, then, is to be done? Must societies be totally abolished? Must meum and tuum be annihilated, and must we return again to the forests to live among the bears? This is a deduction in the manner of my adversaries, which I would as soon anticipate as let them have the shame of drawing. (1972:149)

2 Stephens dryly observes that the needs and rights of children "were not questions explicitly on the agenda of the official Earth Summit, concerned with negotiating phrasing and punctuation in global warming and biodiversity conventions" (Stephens 1992:50).
3 This insight, of course, is not unique to La Farge. In different ways Nancy Chodorow (1978), Barbara Katz Rothman (1989), and Sara Ruddick (1989)

have theorized about the political implications of mothering, as have Marxist feminists writing about social reproduction and gender relations in the family (Dalla Costa 1972; Laslett and Brenner 1989).

2 Selling Environmentalism to Kids

1   The General Agreement on Tariffs and Trade (GATT) is a 108-member international organization that has been in existence since World War II. The Uruguay Round is the latest of a series of GATT multilateral trade negotiations. In these negotiations, nations have been seeking to agree on multilateral rules that govern the commercial importing and exporting of goods. Recent controversy has arisen over proposals to revise the rules and give the GATT new binding powers that would preempt the right of national and local governments to legislate strong environmental protection and other health and safety regulations. If approved, these changes would also extend mandatory deregulation to cover not only goods but services, negatively impacting workers as well as the environment.

2   Meanwhile, as demonstrated in the *Captain Planet* episode described above, so-called developing countries may be depicted as either backward or ignorant of environmental issues, or shortsighted and greedy for Western progress.

3   This is passionately argued by social ecologist Murray Bookchin:

> Liberal environmentalism suffers from a consistent refusal to see that a capitalist society based upon competition and growth for its own sake must ultimately devour the natural world, just like an untreated cancer must ultimately devour its host. Personal intentions, be they good or bad, have little to do with this unrelenting process. An economy that is structured around the maxim, "Grow or Die," must *necessarily* pit itself against the natural world and leave ecological truth in its wake as it works its way through the biosphere. (Bookchin 1990:15)

4   Personal communication with an assistant producer of *Captain Planet,* June 12, 1991.

5   Unless otherwise stated, quotations used here and below are taken from an interview I conducted with an executive producer of *Captain Planet* on July 22, 1991.

3 Children's Concerns about the Planet

1   But see Valerie Walkerdine (1988) for a critique of the notion of "self-managing" citizens and rational democracy in the production of cognitive

reasoning in children. I will explore this question and its relevance to the environmentalization of children in the concluding chapter of this book.

Conclusion

1   Zelig, the central character from Woody Allen's movie of the same name, was notable for his ability to assume many forms in many different situations. I am grateful to Mark Jacobs for providing this apt characterization in informal discussion at the annual meeting of the Society for the Study of Social Problems (SSSP) in Los Angeles, August, 1994.

Bibliography

Adler, Jonathan. 1992. "Little Green Lies: The Environmental Miseducation of America's Children." *Policy Review* (Summer): 18–26.

Ariès, Phillipe. 1962. *Centuries of Childhood.* New York: Random House.

Aufderheide, Pat. 1992. "Media Beat: Do It for the Kids." *In These Times* 16 (40): 19.

Bandy, Joe H. 1992. "Pan/ic Environmentalism: Radical Biocentrism in a Post-natural Era." Master's thesis, University of California, Santa Barbara.

Barber, Benjamin R. 1992. "Jihad vs. McWorld: How the Planet Is Both Falling Apart and Coming Together—and What This Means for Democracy." *The Atlantic* 269 (3): 53–65.

Best, Joel. 1990. *Threatened Children.* Chicago: University of Chicago Press.

Better, Nancy Marx. 1992. "Green Teens." *The New York Times Magazine,* Mar. 8, p. 44.

Bleifuss, Joel. 1994. "The Death of Nations." *In These Times* 18 (16): 12–13.

Boccella, Kathy. 1991. "Kids Are Becoming Proselytizers for the Environment." *Sunday Sun News,* (Myrtle Beach, S.C.), Nov. 24, p. 7C.

Bolotin, Susan. 1990. "Woodman, Spare That Tree!" *The New York Times* (Book Review sec.), May 20, p. 47.

Bookchin, Murray. 1990. *Remaking Society: Pathways to a Green Future.* Boston: South End Press.

Bourdieu, Pierre. 1977. "Cultural Reproduction and Social Reproduction." In Jerome Karabel and A. H. Halsey, eds., *Power and Ideology in Education.* New York: Oxford University Press.

Bullard, Robert. 1990. *Dumping in Dixie: Race, Class, and Environmental Quality.* Boulder, Colo.: Westview Press.

Center for Media Education. 1992. "A Report on Station Compliance with the Children's Television Act." Institute for Public Representation, Georgetown University Law Center, Washington, D.C.

Cherkasova, Maria V. n.d. "Children and Ecologically Related Illnesses in Russia." Center for Independent Ecological Programs/CIEP of the Socio-Ecological Union, Moscow.

Chodorow, Nancy. 1978. *The Reproduction of Mothering.* Berkeley: University of California Press.

Citizen Trade Watch Campaign. 1992. "Environmental, Labor, Consumer, Agricultural, Religious, Citizen's Groups Urge You to Cosponsor the Waxman-Gephardt Resolution Today." Letter to representatives, U.S. Congress, Mar. 5.

Coles, Robert. 1986. *The Moral Life of Children.* Boston: Atlantic Monthly Press.

————. 1992. *Their Eyes Meeting the World: The Drawings and Paintings of Children.* Burlington, Mass.: Houghton Mifflin.

Colletti, Lucio. 1972. *From Rousseau to Lenin: Studies in Ideology and Society.* New York: Monthly Review Press.

Coward, Rosalind. 1990. "Greening the Child." *New Statesman and Society* 102 (3): 40–41.

Dalla Costa, Mariarosa. 1972. *The Power of Women and the Subversion of the Community.* Bristol, U.K.: Falling Wall Press.

Dawkins, Kristin. 1992. "Global Trade Pact: A Bad Deal for Women." *Toward Freedom* 1 (2): 9–10.

de Beauvoir, Simone. 1952. *The Second Sex.* New York: Knopf.

Diamond, Irene, and Gloria Feman Orenstein, eds. 1990. *Reweaving the World: The Emergence of Ecofeminism.* San Francisco: Sierra Club Books.

Engelhardt, Tom. 1987. "The Shortcake Strategy." In Todd Gitlin, ed., *Watching Television.* New York: Pantheon.

Firestone, Shulamith. 1970. *The Dialectic of Sex.* New York: Bantam.

Fischoff, Baruch. 1991. "Report from Poland: Science and Politics in the Midst of Disaster." *Environment* 33 (2): 12–37.

Foucault, Michel. 1980. *Power/Knowledge.* New York: Pantheon.

Garelik, Glenn. 1991. "The Enforcers: Teach Your Parents Well." *USA Weekend Magazine,* Aug. 9–11, pp. 4–5.

Glaser, Nathan, and Anselm Strauss. 1967. *The Discovery of Grounded Theory.* Hawthorne, N.Y.: Aldine de Gruyter.

Goldman, Benjamin A. 1992. "Alternative Summit Echoes U.N. Conference's Problems." *In These Times* 28 (16): 10–11.

Goldman, Benjamin A., and Lois M. Goldman. 1992. "At a Summit Filled with Empty Rhetoric, Cuba Produces a Glowing Agreement." *In These Times* 28 (16): 11.

Gore, Jennifer. 1992. "What We Can Do for You! What *Can* "We" Do for "You"? Struggling over Empowerment in Critical and Feminist Pedagogy." In Carmen Luke and Jennifer Gore, eds., *Feminisms and Critical Pedagogy.* New York: Routledge.

Gutin, JoAnn. 1992. "Plastics-a-Go-Go: The Joy of Making New Useless Junk out of Old Useless Junk." *Mother Jones* 17 (2): 56–59.

Hall, Stuart. 1981. "Notes on Deconstructing the Popular." In R. Samuel, ed., *People's History and Socialist Theory.* London: Routledge and Kegan Paul.

Haraway, Donna. 1992. "The Promises of Monsters: A Regenerative Politics for Inappropriate/d Others." In Lawrence Grossberg, Cary Nelson, and Paula Treichler, eds., *Cultural Studies.* New York: Routledge.

Hess, Robert D. 1968. "Political Socialization in the Schools." *Harvard Educational Review* 38 (3): 528–36.

Hicks, Stephen R. C. 1991. "Let Kids Be Kids." *Wall Street Journal,* Apr. 16, p. A20.

Hirsh, Liz. 1994. "Halflife." *The Progressive* 58 (7): 39.

"Home Street, U.S.A.: People Living with Pollution." 1991. *Greenpeace,* Oct.–Dec., pp. 8–13.

Kellner, Douglas. 1987. "TV, Ideology, and Emancipatory Popular Culture." In Horace Newcombe, ed., *Television: The Critical View.* New York: Oxford University Press.

King, Donna Lee. 1994. "Using Children's Drawings in Sociological Research." Paper presented at the annual meeting of the American Sociological Association, Los Angeles, Calif., Aug. 5–9.

King, Ynestra. 1990. "Healing the Wounds: Feminism, Ecology, and the Nature/Culture Dualism." In Irene Diamond and Gloria Feman Orenstein, eds., *Reweaving the World.* San Francisco: Sierra Club Books.

Kline, Stephen. 1993. *Out of the Garden: Toys and Children's Culture in the Age of TV Marketing.* London: Verso.

La Farge, Phyllis. 1987. *The Strangelove Legacy: The Impact of Nuclear Threat on Children.* New York: Harper and Row.

Laslett, Barbara, and Johanna Brenner. 1989. "Gender and Social Reproduction: Historical Perspectives." *Annual Sociological Review* 15:381–404.

Le Guin, Ursula K. 1982. *The Language of the Night.* New York: Berkeley Books.

Luke, Carmen. 1992. "Feminist Politics in Radical Pedagogy." In Carmen Luke and Jennifer Gore, eds., *Feminisms and Critical Pedagogy.* New York: Routledge.

Lynott, Patricia Passuth, and Barbara J. Logue. 1993. "The 'Hurried Child': The Myth of Lost Childhood in Contemporary American Society." *Sociological Forum* 8 (3): 471–491.

McNeal, James U. 1992. *Kids as Customers.* New York: Lexington Books.

Mesnikoff, Wendy Savin. 1989. "The Place of Nuclear Threat in Young People's Everyday Concerns and Expectations." Ph.D. diss., Graduate Center, City University of New York.

New York Times Magazine. 1992. Letters to the editor. May 13, p. 6.

Ortner, Sherry. 1974. "Is Female to Male as Nature Is to Culture?" In Michelle Z. Rosaldo and Louise Lamphere, eds. *Women, Culture and Society.* Stanford, Calif.: Stanford University Press.

Palonsky, Stuart B. 1987. "Political Socialization in Elementary Schools." *Elementary School Journal* 87 (5): 492–505.

Postman, Neil. 1985. *Amusing Ourselves to Death.* New York: Viking.

Quindlen, Anna. 1990. "Thou Shalt Nots." *New York Times,* Oct. 14, sec. E.

Rosenthal, Paul C. 1992. "A Lose–Lose Trade Bargain? How the Democrats Could Turn GATT into a Hot Campaign Issue." *Washington Post,* Feb. 16.

Rothman, Barbara Katz. 1989. *Recreating Motherhood: Ideology and Technology in a Patriarchal Society.* New York: Norton.

———. 1993. "The Active Management of Physicians." *Birth* 20 (3) (Sept.): 158–59.

———. 1994. Presidential address to the annual meeting of the Society for the Study of Social Problems, Los Angeles, Calif., Aug. 5.

Ruddick, Sara. 1989. *Maternal Thinking: Towards a Politics of Peace.* New York: Ballantine Books.

Seager, Joni. 1993. *Earth Follies: Coming to Feminist Terms with the Environmental Crisis.* New York: Routledge.

Seiter, Ellen. 1993. *Sold Separately: Parents and Children in Consumer Culture.* New Brunswick, N.J.: Rutgers University Press.

Shahin, Jim. 1994. "Parenting in the Nineties: The Winds of Ecological, Dietary, and Social Change Have Transformed Parenting. Haven't They?" *American Way,* Mar. 1, pp. 30–34.

Simonds, Wendy, and Barbara Katz Rothman. 1992. *Centuries of Solace: Expressions of Maternal Grief in Popular Literature.* Philadelphia: Temple University Press.

Singer, Daniel. 1994. "Does the Left Have a Future?" *The Nation* 259 (4): 122–25.

Slesin, Suzanne. 1991. "Newest Parental Nightmare: Eco-smart child." *New York Times* (Home sec.), July 11, sec. C.

Stephens, Sharon. 1992. "Children and the UN Conference on Environment and Development: Participants and Media Symbols." *Barn/Research on Children in Norway* (2–3): 44–52.

———. 1994. "Children and Environment: Local Worlds and Global Connections." *Childhood* 2 (1/2): 1–21.

———. 1995. *Children and the Politics of Culture: Risks, Rights and Reconstructions.* Princeton, N.J.: Princeton University Press.

TBS Productions, Inc., and DIC Enterprises, Inc. 1990. "Captain Planet and the Planeteers: The Power Is Yours." Public relations kit.

"Toxic Ten: America's Truant Corporations." 1993. *Mother Jones,* Jan.–Feb., pp. 39–42.

Turner, Jack. 1994. "The Practice of the Wild: A Gary Synder Primer." *Patagonia Winter Catalog.*

U.S. Environmental and Consumer Groups. 1992. "The Dec. 20, 1991 GATT Uruguay Round 'Final Act' Must Be Rejected." Letter to representatives, U.S. Congress, Jan. 9.

USA Weekend Magazine. 1991. Letters to the editor, Oct. 4–6: p. 18.

Walkerdine, Valerie. 1988. *The Mastery of Reason.* London: Routledge.

———. 1992. "Progressive Pedagogy and Political Struggle." In Carmen Luke and Jennifer Gore, eds., *Feminisms and Critical Pedagogy.* New York: Routledge.

Walters, Robert. 1992. "Poison in the Pacific." *The Progressive* 56 (7): 32–35.

Watterson, Bill. 1994. "Calvin and Hobbes." *Wilmington Sunday Star–News* (Wilmington, N.C.), Mar. 13.

Wiener, Don. 1992. "Will GATT Negotiations Trade Away the Future?" *In These Times* (Feb. 12–18): 7.

Wright, H. B. 1991. Editorial cartoon. *Palm Beach Post,* Aug. 11, p. 12.

Yarrow, Leon. 1960. "Interviewing Children." In Paul Mussen, ed., *Handbook of Research Methods in Child Development.* New York: Wiley.

Yasi, Jenny Ruth. 1993. "Save the Earth?" *Mothering,* Fall.

Zelizer, Viviana A. 1985. *Pricing the Priceless Child: The Changing Social Value of Children.* New York: Basic Books.

INDEX

abortion, child's view of,
80–81
Adler, Jonathan, 8, 20–21,
105, 114
adult-like children, 21–22
animals, children's concern
for, 61–62, 75, 77, 88
antinuclear movement, children's roles in, 18
Ariès, Phillipe, 10, 11, 12

Bookchin, Murray, 40, 107–
108, 113, 124n3
Bourdieu, Pierre, 117
Brazilian street children: and
Earth Summit, 14; radioac-
tive contamination of, 15
Building Bombs, 17

Calvin and Hobbes, 20
*Captain Planet and the
Planeteers,* 4, 30, 36–50,
51, 71, 84, 97, 111, 117,
124n2, 124n4, 124n5; children's views of, 42–44,
45, 47–48, 55
cartoon themes, gender differences in, 52, 63

Centuries of Childhood
(Ariès), 10
Cherkasova, Marie V., 7
children's drawings as research method, 56–58
children's environmental concerns: adult views of, 55–
56; calling for action, 58,
59, 64–66; depicting the
problem, 58, 59, 66–68;
everything's okay, 58, 59–
61; indicting the problem
makers, 58, 59, 68–70;
race, class, and gender differences in, 67–68, 69–70;
recasting the problem, 58,
59, 70–71; taking personal
action, 58, 59, 61–64
children's feelings about environmental crisis, 82–91
children's images in environmental crisis, 7–27; dur-
ing Earth Summit, 13–14;
as ecotyrants, 4, 8–9,
22–27, 56; as endangered
species, 8, 15–16; as little
animals and noble savages,
4, 7, 11–15; as political
pawns, 4, 8, 20–21, 26,

children's images in environmental crisis (*continued*) 27, 102–103, 105; as vulnerable victims, 4, 16–18, 19–20, 21, 55–56
children's television, deregulation of, 38–39
Children's Television Act (1990), 39
Ciba-Geigy, 16
Colletti, Lucio, 12, 123n1
consumer culture, children's, 51–53
consumer market, children as, 116
corporate greed, 33, 35, 50
Coward, Rosalind, 1, 51, 52–53
crisis themes, generations of, 1

diffusion of responsibility, children's experience of, 90, 91–96
disappearance of childhood, 10, 11
discovery of childhood, 10–11

Earth Summit, children's rights and, 111, 112, 123n2
ecofeminism, 119
ecological well-being, children's, 19
Engelhardt, Tom, 38–39, 42, 52, 71
environmental activism, children's: as conflict-free, 51; conservative views on, 20–21, 26, 27, 102–103, 105; as hard work, 62; liberal views on, 21, 26–27
environmental education: as political indoctrination, 8, 20–21
environmental empowerment: critique of, 5, 117–121; meaning for children, 96–114
environmental essay contest, 2
environmental overload, 19–20
environmental racism, 16
environmental risk, children's, 15–16
Exxon Valdez, children's drawings of, 69; child's view of, 94

Ferngully: The Last Rainforest, 34–35, 50, 113
50 Simple Things Kids Can Do to Save the Earth (Javna), 2
Foucault, Michel, 118

Gaia (UNICEF ship), 13, 14
Gaia: as cartoon character, 45–47; as nature, 45–47
garbage, children's views of, 75–78
garbage police, 85
GATT (General Agreement on Tariffs and Trade), 40, 124n1
Global Forum, children's frustration at, 111–112
global management, 39–40

Gore, Jennifer, 118
green advertising, 27, 111
Green party (Germany), 3
green teens, 27
Gutin, JoAnn, 85, 95

Haraway, Donna, 120
Herman, Pee Wee, 21–22
Hess, Robert, 115–116

inspiration of the child, 18

Just a Dream (Van Allsburg),
    31–32, 50

Kellner, Douglas, 81, 106
Kline, Stephen, 51–52

La Farge, Phyllis, 18, 56,
    123n3
LeGuin, Ursula, 113
letter-writing to politicians,
    children's, 101–103, 114
liberal environmental para-
    dox, 4, 30, 36, 38, 39, 40,
    48–50, 90–91, 105–106,
    117, 119
licensed character products,
    38–39, 51–52
lifestyle solutions, 2–3, 26,
    27, 51, 53, 116
Lorax, The (Dr. Suess), 32–
    33

Moore, Michael, 11–12
mothering as political action,
    18, 123–124n3
multinational corporations,
    49–50, 117; children's
    lack of awareness of, 94.

See also transnational cor-
    porations

nature as mother and re-
    source, 40, 41, 45–47,
    119
1960s generation parents, 24
nuclear nightmares, 1, 56
nuclear overload, 56

overpopulation: children's
    views of, 79–81; racist rep-
    resentations of, 13–14, 81
ozone hole, children's view
    of, 77–78, 83, 88

Pee Wee Herman, 21–22
political socialization, 115–
    116
Postman, Neil, 110
psychic numbing, 1, 56

recycling, children's views
    of, 76–77, 84–85, 95
Roger & Me, 11–12
Rothman, Barbara Katz, 11,
    35, 40, 119, 123n3
Rousseau, Jean Jacques, 12,
    123n1
Russia, children's health con-
    ditions, 8

Seager, Joni, 16
seed of life, feminist critique
    of, 35
Seiter, Ellen, 52, 63
Snyder, Gary, 7
social reproduction, 4
Stephens, Sharon, 14, 111,
    112, 123n2

transnational corporations, 40; international monitoring of, 33–34

U.S. Atomic Energy Commission, 14–15

Waldorf school, 107

Walkerdine, Valerie, 121, 124n1
Wright, Steve, 19

Yarrow, Leon, 82, 83

Zelizer, Vivianna, 10

ABOUT THE AUTHOR

Donna Lee King is a professor of sociology at the University of North Carolina at Wilmington.